Smoothies!

The Original Smoothie Book
Recipes From the Pro's

Dan Titus

Published by Juice Gallery Multimedia

OTHER BOOKS BY THE AUTHOR

The Juice & Smoothie Bar Business Plan

The Smoothie Kiosk Business Plan

The Mobile Juice & Smoothie Bar Business Plan

The Juice & Smoothie Industry Analysis

The Smoothie Cookbook Professional

The Juice & Smoothie Bar Operations Manual

The Wrap Store Business Plan

The Coffee House Business Plan

The Koffee Kiosk Business Plan

The Bagel Store Business Plan

That's a Wrap! Sandwich and Soup Recipe Book

Acknowledgments

This book couldn't have been written without the support of the many players in the juice and smoothie industry. Players, such as: retail juice and smoothie companies, manufacturing companies, distribution companies, media companies and most importantly smoothie lovers. These *players* have banded together to form a grassroots movement that has become known as the juice & smoothie industry.

Kudos to Steven Kuhnau, who promoted the word *smoothie* into a household drink name. Thanks to Kirk Perron, who married fresh squeezed juice and smoothies into a distinctive California offering. Thanks to early adopters: Larry Sidoti, Susan Jesperson, Martin Sprock, Eric Strauss and David Robertson for believing in their dreams, and therefore moving the industry forward to a generic name.

Appreciation to Ken Smith for his tireless distribution efforts and faith in the industry, and to Mike and Ellen Walsh for their early media support.

To smoothie lovers, of all ages, worldwide: **You're Too Cool!**

For Tania, our little queen

Table of Contents

Foreword

Congratulations! You hold in your hand the key to making professional smoothies: **Smoothies! - The Original Smoothie Book, Recipes From The Pro's.**

Why do we call it the original smoothie book?

The answer: Because professionals in the juice and smoothie industry contributed to its creation.

All recipes within this book have been time-tested over years and years. Millions of smoothies have been served using the smoothie recipes contained in this book.

Within the pages that follow, we will provide you with professional recipes of the kind used in real juice & smoothie bars. Yes, you will be able to make smoothies just like the pro's in the privacy of your own kitchen!

Smoothies! The Original Smoothie Book
Recipes From The Pro's

The demand for fresh quality food alternatives is driving the current wave of health orientated consumers to seek places to purchase products that meet their discriminating tastes. This is evidenced by the rapid increase in holistic and natural food stores and more recently, the proliferation of specialized restaurants and juice stores.

The medical establishment and the government have become aware of the health benefits of natural foods. The National Cancer Institute advocates serving foods that are fresh and uncooked in order preserve vitamin content. The American Medical Association continues to study fresh foods for vitamin content and more recently, is engaged in studies of natural herbs to find out what chemicals in them remedy ailments.

Throughout the decade's health crazes have come and gone. However, as consumers are educated and learn more about ways to juice and prepare natural recipes at home, the current trend in healthy eating will soon establish itself as a mainstay. As consumers demand for healthy meal alternatives mature, more and more retail outlets will open to satisfy demand.

Smoothies! The Original Smoothie Book - Recipes From The Pro's has been written to educate you about the juice and smoothie business. The book provides a historical overview of the juice and smoothie industry. It has been written to help people learn about some of the recipes and procedures required to successfully prepare smoothies and fresh squeezed juices at home.

Why a Juice or Smoothie?

Smoothies! The Original Smoothie Book
Recipes From The Pro's

Ever yawn after that big lunch you just ate? Ever run for a cup of coffee in the afternoon just to keep yourself going? Well, I have. That is I used to, until I discovered the secret to keeping myself on the go.

I learned years ago that I could change the way I eat. I learned that if I ate more raw fruits and vegetables, I would in general, feel better, and at the same time increase my energy level. I learned to eat raw fruits and vegetables more frequently throughout the day. Instead of having my traditional bowl of cereal for breakfast, I would eat a sweet juicy navel orange. Instead of having a hamburger for lunch, I would skip it, and have a salad instead. In between meals I'd snack on a few raw nuts and sunflower seeds. I'd have more fruit, vegetables, or maybe some raw carrots and celery. The key for me was less, more frequently. However, I found that sometimes I'd be in a situation where I couldn't snack and then, I'd go hungry. I needed a way to get my intake of raw fruits and vegetables quickly. The answer: Juice 'um.

I bought a large Champion juicer and started juicing carrots. Then, I got brave and added some garlic and onion. Whooooo, potent stuff! Maybe some beets and parsley? That tastes...cool-daddy-O-baby-I-want-cha! What I had inadvertently created was a prelude to the "veggie-combo" pure vegetable drink. I'd pour this stuff in my thermos, and it was "...off to work we go." I no longer had to snack as frequently. I simple drank my breakfast and lunch. I had more energy than ever before. Why? Because my body would quickly assimilate all the nutrition. It didn't have to work so hard by spending energy digesting and processing what I had just consumed.

Smoothies! The Original Smoothie Book
Recipes From The Pro's

Many of us simple do not eat raw fruits and vegetables. We rely on a diet, which consists of large amounts of animal fat: cheeseburgers, fried chicken, steaks, pizza, and meat-filled sandwiches. We load on the unhealthy snack foods too, such as cookies and ice cream. All this junk food, which has excess fat, is hard for the body to digest. This will slow you down and make you tired.

Fruits and vegetables give you fuel for fitness. They provide carbohydrates, the body's preferable source for energy, with little fat. They have no cholesterol. Many are naturally low in calories and sodium. Some are good sources of potassium, which is an electrolyte used by muscles. Basically, fruits and vegetables are the stuff life is made of. So eat as many as you can, when you can. Get yourself a juicer and juice 'um and drink 'um. Or for a tasty meal alternative or treat, make yourself a smoothie. It is the healthy choice that will be sure to put a smile on your face for breakfast, lunch, dinner, or that snack in between.

Over the past few years juice and smoothie bars have been popping up all over the country with the primary objective of offering the public an alternative to most fast foods. Menu items range from fresh squeezed juice, to bagels, to coffee. However, the main item sold is the fruit juice smoothie.

The fruit juice smoothie has been positioned in many juice and smoothie bars as a healthy meal in a cup. Smoothies are easily digested, and therefore won't bog you down after you drink it.

The basic ingredients in a smoothie are: fruit juice, ice milk or frozen yogurt, fruit, and crushed ice. Also, many juice and smoothie bars add vitamin supplements to the drinks. These are usually in the form of two free supplements that you have the choice of, with additional supplements costing more. Sounds simple enough? The secret is knowing what the portions are.

To start making smoothies at home, go to the "Quick Recipes" section. This will allow you to get started right away.

Get creative and make your own smoothie recipes. Share them with family and friends. And above all, have fun!

Follow the recipes in this book, and you will be making smoothies at home, just like the professionals!

Vitality for Life and Body...
...Get healthy. Stay healthy.

Enjoy!

Dan "The Smoothieman" Titus

History

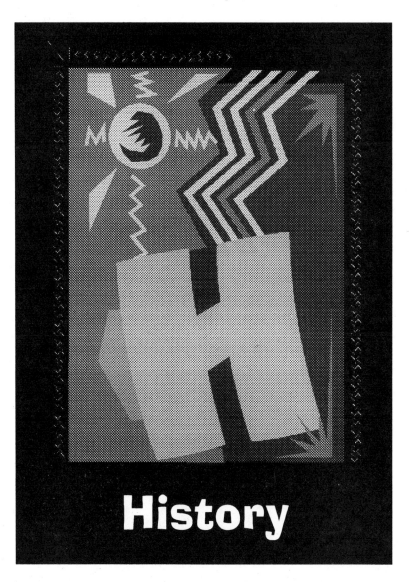

The dictionaries of the world are behind the times when defining the word smoothie. I am sure this will change in the next few years.

Merriam-Webster Dictionary™

Smoothie

- Main Entry: **smoothy**
  Variant(s): *or* **smooth·ie** / ' smü – [<u>th</u>] E/
  Function: ***noun***
  Inflected Form(s): *plural* **smooth·ies**
  Date: 1904
  1. a smooth-tongued person
  2. a person with polished manners b: one who behaves or performs with deftness, assurance, and easy competence; *especially* : a man with an ingratiating manner toward women.

- Noun: someone with an assured and ingratiating manner [syn: **smoothy**, sweet talker charmer.

As evidenced above, the word smoothie dates back to the early 1900's. This is the first published definition of the word; however, it can be assumed that the word had been part of the American vocabulary for many years prior to this.
The words *smoothie, smoothy* and *smoothee* go as far back as the early 1930's. The word smoothie was used first by the Adler Company of Connecticut in 1932 as a trade name for the company's line of foundation garments, namely, girdles and brassieres. Therefore, the first legal references to these words did not have anything to do with drinks or foods at all until a few years later.

Smoothies! The Original Smoothie Book
Recipes From The Pro's

Bowey's Incorporated of Indianapolis, Indiana, marketed a chocolate syrup for food purposes, and a powder for making chocolate syrup in 1935. This is the first reference to drinks for the words. There is even a song from this period called, *You're an Old Smoothie*. The words continued to be used for many other trade purposes.

The word smoothie was used as a trade name for a brand of automotive paints in the late 1950's. It was also used as a trade name for a manufacturer who made caps, gloves and bathing suits. Also, at that time, there was a manufacturer who made electrical components who used the word smoothie as a trade name for switches and wall plates. The word continued to evolve.

The tropical regions of South America are traditionally the fruit capitals of the world. Brazil is the largest supplier of these fruits in the world; it is the fruit juice capital, too. Natives have known about the benefits of juice for centuries and have included it as a staple in their diet.

Latin Americans, with their rich supply of exotic fruits, have enjoyed the benefits of juicing for years. I can remember as a boy vacationing along the Baja coast of Mexico in the late 1950's, finding tiny thatched juice bars right on the beach!

Smoothies became popular in the middle 1960's, when there was a resurgence in the United States in macrobiotic vegetarianism. Retail health restaurants literally sprouted up to cater to the demand. One of the popular menu items was the fruit juice smoothie. California, one of the focal points of this trend, borrowed the venerable fruit juice smoothie from its South American neighbors.

Smoothies! The Original Smoothie Book
Recipes From The Pro's

In 1969 there was a trademark registered for the name "Cream Smoothie", this, in reference to a soft drink line. The first reference to a fruit slush came in the middle 1970's with the name California Smoothie, which was claimed by California Smoothie Company of Paramus New Jersey. Mr. Smoothie, of Houston, Texas, used the name in, "Famous Mr. Smoothie's Frozen Yogurt" since the early 1980's.

The word smoothie has been used to describe many products over the years. From bicycles, girdles, to ball point pens. There is even a popular band called the *Smoothies*. However, the word, in relation to the frozen beverage industry did not really become generic until Smoothie King of Kenner, Louisiana, made the word a household name.

The smoothies of old differed by today's standards in that, at that time, most did not have ice milk, or frozen yogurt in them. They were basically fruit, fruit juice, and ice. The idea of adding vitamin supplements had not taken shape yet. By the early 1970's, ice milk had been commandeered to make what then was known as the fruit shake. These shakes were served at local health-food restaurants and within health-food stores.

The 1970's, with its earth-tone decor of natural colors, was the renaissance decade for natural health food stores and restaurants. National Universities touted the warnings of a fragile environment to students, who took the heed to help protect the environment and their own bodies. The word *natural* was the marketing battle cry of many national brands of foods, from breakfast cereals to carbonated soda drinks. Along with the long hair and "earth-shoes", came the proliferation of "health restaurants". I can remember Main Street, Huntington Beach, California, with the head shops, and the Tofu and Smoothie Bars. There is one still there to this day, serving avocado, alfalfa sprout sandwiches and fresh squeezed carrot juice, and of course, fruit juice smoothies.

In the early 1970's, Stephen Kuhnau, Smoothie King cofounder, called his "smoothies" energy drinks in order to describe his product to customers. "I didn't invent the word smoothie. The first time I heard the word was in reference to fruit and fruit juice based drinks made by the "Hippies" in the late 1960's. Since then, I have always been on the look out as to where the name smoothie originated. To date, I have seen old black and white movies where a "cool gent" is described as a smoothy, and even reference to a brand of cigarettes called smoothies." Enter the 1980's.

"Yuppie malts and yuppie doughnuts describe smoothies and bagels in the late 1980's."

The sports and fitness trends were beginning to catch on in the early 1980's. With these trends, came the increased awareness of natural foods. Marketers began to openly market "calcium" and "oat-bran" as supplements to their products. This ushered in the beginning to the first specialized juice and smoothie bars, which are increasing in popularity today.

"In the 1990's the smoothie evolves into the truly politically correct shake."

In the 1990's, with the growing interest in good health and convenience, juice and smoothie bars were experiencing rapid growth as more and more people were introduced to the concept of healthy meal alternatives. The 1990's emerged as a decade of maturation for the fitness movement, marked by consumer interest in diet and exercise. A simultaneous counter-trend has been the acceleration of the fast-food craze. This, evidenced by the consumers' demand for healthy convenient meal alternatives. The juice and smoothie bar industry will be frozen yogurt business of the 2000's.

Leaving behind the politically correct" nineties...

> *"In the 2000's the smoothie emerges as the whimsical beverage recognized for its health benefits worldwide."*

The juice and smoothie industry is a multi-billion dollar industry. The number of juice and smoothie bars has skyrocketed and retail stores can now be found throughout the world. Stores are beginning to sprout-up on school campuses, in airports, and generally anywhere people congregate. The concept has really gone full circle, as evidenced by Wild Oats, the nations largest natural health-food chain, providing cyber-juice bars inside all of their store locations. This is a throwback to the 1970's model where juice and smoothie bars were a sideline to the natural health-food store. This concept echoes the recent trends in the coffeehouse business, whereby computer terminals with access to the internet are provided for customer use.

People like choices. They demand products that appeal to their needs and wants for a healthier life style. What can be simpler than a smoothie? It's good for you and has zero fat. It's a healthy meal in a cup. It's a treat. It's a snack. It tastes great!

Therefore, we continue to see the gradual development the smoothie. From its formidable beginnings in South America, as basically a fruit slush, to the most recent incarnation as the power drink for the future. Juice & smoothie bars will continue to proliferate as demand for meal alternatives broadens.

Definitions of Juice & Smoothie Bars and Stores

Juice Bar – Retail quick-service restaurant operation that specializes in fruit juice smoothies and fresh-squeezed juice. Products in this category are positioned as a meal replacement or meal enhancement to healthy snacks and/or meals served in the store.

Smoothie Store – Retail quick-service restaurant that specializes in fruit juice smoothies and *no* fresh-squeezed juice. Products in this category are primarily positioned as a meal replacement and/or a dessert.

Frozen Dessert Store – Retail ice cream and/or frozen yogurt store, which specializes in frozen desserts. Fruit juice smoothies served in this category are positioned primarily as a dessert offering.

Smoothie Mixes or Starter Bases – Wholesale products offered mainly to existing retail food service operations that wish to diversify menu offering to include fruit juice smoothie products. These products are positioned as a meal enhancement and/or as an after meal dessert.

Industry Blueprints

The West Coast

In the true definition of a *California Juice & Smoothie Bar*, the first Juice Club opened in April 1990 at San Luis Obispo, California. This industry flagship for the west coast introduced a new concept to local college students eager to embrace fruit juice smoothies, fresh squeezed juice, and healthy snacks. The success of this store set the stage for expansion.

The awareness of the juice bar phenomenon became evident when Juice Club opened a franchise store in 1993, in Irvine, California. The store, located on the corner of Harvard and Main streets in a local shopping center, became an instant icon. The location is perfect! It is located between University of California, Irvine, and John Wayne Airport. The area around the airport sports a huge business complex. The location provided the necessary demographic base for instant success, exemplified by frequent visits by college students and local business people.

The Harvard and Main Street location planted the seed for the proliferation of the juice bar industry in Southern California. Business people and college students who frequented the location saw the upside potential of the concept, and began to emulate the idea. For example, upstarts like Juice Stop opened their first store in nearby Lake Forest in December, 1993. Juice it Up! opened their first store in Brea, an inland Southern California community with similar demographics to Irvine, in March,1995. Both companies are successful players in the industry today.

The Southeast

Industry veteran, Smoothie King, is a New Orleans-based chain, that began franchising in 1989. They define the concept in regards to the smoothie store concept because they offer only fruit juice smoothies, nutritional products and supplements.

There are many emulators in this segment, the most notables: Planet Smoothie, based in Atlanta, Georgia, and Frozen Fusion, based in Scottsdale, Arizona.

It is interesting to note, that for the most part, you will find juice bars on the West Coast and smoothie stores in the southern portions of the United States. This points to the direct correlation with industry blueprint influences, which generally set standards for a particular region.

Therefore, the specialty juice and smoothie concept has been around for almost 20 years. But, not until the middle 1990's, did the consumer awareness for the products increase. This is attributed primarily to consumer demand for healthy meal alternatives and to the sheer number of specialty stores popping up across the country, thereby introducing and educating people about the industry.

Consumers, with their driving requests for a healthier meal alternative, have been eager to embrace the juice and smoothies. Restaurants now offer low calorie and salt free menu offerings to patrons. Why not add juice and/or smoothies? Many, in the future, will begin to offer fruit juice smoothies and juices as menu offerings.

Smoothies! The Original Smoothie Book
Recipes From The Pro's

New entrants into the juice and smoothie business include many existing franchise companies, such as sandwich chains, existing yogurt companies, and convenience stores. The basic strategy has been to create a brand name that can be co-branded and offered to existing franchisees already in the retail channel. This is evidenced by companies such as: Subway Corporation, 7-Eleven's Frut Cooler Brand and Blimpie International's Smoothie Island Brand.

As the juice and smoothie industry matures we will undoubtedly see more of this as more established restaurant franchisers scramble to capitalize on this growing trend. This causes a "blurring of lines" for the traditional juice and smoothie bar. The question: Is the smoothie being offered as a concept or menu item?

Smoothies have been around for years as a simple menu item, and then the product became a branded concept, which ushered in the first specialized retail juice and smoothie bars. As more established restaurant chains jump into the juice and smoothie business, they have a choice to develop their own brand of smoothies or obtain an established brand already in the marketplace.

Recently, co-branding has been prevalent in the juice smoothie business; however, these co-brands, at this time, are not established and it will be an expensive endeavor to entrench these brand names into the marketplace. We all know the pull of a powerful brand name. Look at the power of Coca-Cola as a menu item. Building a brand name is difficult and costly.

There are dominate regional brand names in the juice and smoothie retail segment, such as Jamba Juice and Smoothie King. These are basically the leaders that many established franchise chains have chosen to emulate. The question is: How do you emulate a whole juice and smoothie bar concept with just a menu item and at the same time, stave off the dominate retail juice/smoothie bar concept brands when competition heats up as the industry matures?

Care must be taken at every turn of the marketing process and companies have to know how to position their smoothie products in the marketplace. This is critical. Is the product offered as a:

- Meal replacement
- Meal enhancement
- Dessert

For the most part, stand-alone retail juice and smoothie stores position themselves as meal replacement and/or meal enhancement. Yogurt and established frozen dessert stores position their smoothies as dessert offerings.

When you go out for a smoothie, be aware of how the store is offering the smoothie. Read more about smoothie definitions later in the "Smoothie Definitions" section.

The juice and smoothie business continues to evolve. We have seen the original concepts change in recent years, whereby companies have added specialty restaurant items to their menus. For example, gourmet coffee, salads, sandwiches, wrap sandwiches and bagels have become popular offerings. Some chain's have even developed. Worldwraps of San Francisco serves wrap sandwiches and smoothies. Many coffee houses offer juice and smoothies and bagels, too. Therefore, we are seeing "traditional" specialty and co-branding concepts merging together under one roof.

Smoothie Definitions

Defining A Smoothie

Recently, the word smoothie has been used to describe many different kinds of beverage drinks. Several manufactures have used the word to describe their packaged drink products, even though the beverages do not contain any real juice or fresh ingredients! This leads to confusion and devalues the name smoothie. Let's attempt to dispel any confusion about the definition(s) of a smoothie. A fruit smoothie can have anything in it. Just put the contents into a high speed blender, hit the switch, and if the contents come out smooth, you have a smoothie. This is what makes defining a smoothie so difficult. Therefore, some clarification is needed.

There seems to be a lot of confusion as to what a smoothie really is. I came up with this simple ranking system which defines a smoothie by using decision criterion.
Since smoothies are associated with health, and health and fitness are associated with the Olympics, I decided to use the metals platinum, gold, silver, and bronze to rank the different levels of smoothies. Below you will find questions asked when defining a smoothie.

Platinum Smoothie

- Is the smoothie made to order using fresh ingredients?
- Is fresh squeezed juice used?
- Is the fruit freshly cut?
- Are both of these items organic?
- High marks for any smoothie made to order and prepared with all natural ingredients. Freshly squeezed juice and real fresh fruit make for a top ranked smoothie.

Gold Smoothie

- Is the smoothie made with any combination of fresh or 100% juice concentrates, and/or (IQF - 100% real frozen fruit) produce and made to order?
- High marks for a smoothie made to order using seasonal fruit or 100% frozen fruit and 100% fruit juice from concentrates.

The 2000's rendition of a professional smoothie recipe is: Fruit juice, fruit, crushed ice, and/or non-fat frozen yogurt or sherbet. The product is generally *made to order within a specialty juice and smoothie bar* and blended in a high speed blender. Vitamin supplements are added at the discretion of the customer. The customer usually can see the custom made product right before their eyes. Note that a smoothie in this category can be made at home, if it is made using the appropriate recipe.

Domestic smoothies contain a wide variety of ingredients and do not fall within the definition of a professional smoothie. These smoothie recipes are generally created by people at home for personal use to share with family and friends. If you make your smoothies at home and within the definitions outlined above, you will create a Platinum or Gold level smoothie. If you don't, your smoothie will fall in one of the other smoothie categories.

Silver Smoothie

- Is the smoothie made from a starter mix or other proprietary smoothie base, which uses 100% natural ingredients?
- This ranking is based on the ingredients that make up the smoothie mix or starter base. Basically, if the contents are high quality, in the way of 100% fruit purees and fruit juice, they qualify as a silver smoothie.

This product is generally served via a dispenser machine, similar to softserve ice-cream, or blended in a high speed blender. The product is easily added to an existing menu because it does not require the equipment and expense that is necessary to prepare a custom made smoothie. This product can generally be made at home using a high-speed blender, if you have the smoothie mix or starter base.

Bronze Smoothie

- Is the smoothie made from a prepackaged smoothie mix or is product that is *not* 100% natural?
- Is the smoothie prepackage and consumed out of a container?
- Any smoothie that does not contain natural ingredients falls in this category. Also, *ready-to-drink* smoothies found in grocery stores fall into this category.

Smoothies in cans and prepackaged containers are generally available through grocery stores and local markets.

Profiles of Juice & Smoothie Bar Companies

Profiles

Crazy Carrot
St. Paul Minnesota

When the Crazy Carrot Juice Bar arrived in a neighborhood in Saint Paul in January, 1998, the seeds were sown for rapid success. In business for less than six months, the company's first location has been known to use more than 3,000 pounds of oranges a week, up to 1,500 pounds of jumbo carrots, and hundreds of pounds of bananas, strawberries, raspberries, and other assorted fruits and vegetables.

The Crazy Carrot's ingredients were carefully conceived and orchestrated by members of 'Team Carrot' - a group of people strategically put together to take the company to the next level. The Crazy Carrot concept - which consists of everything from the distinctive logo, to the end-of-a-kind smoothies, to the company's focus on environmental awareness - was more than eighteen months in the planning.

Beginning in 1996, CEO Eric Strauss and other members of "Team Carrot", began scouring the country for juice bars. From California to Florida, Eric visited more than one hundred juice and smoothie bars in his quest to perfect the Crazy Carrot concept. Studying every aspect of a juice bar's operation, Eric soon honed in on the ultimate juice bar prototype.

By September, 1998, the second Crazy Carrot had opened for business in Minneapolis' hip Uptown neighborhood. Shortly thereafter, in October, 1998, the company opened their third location near the University of Minnesota. Two additional locations opened for business in Spring, 1999. Are there other Crazy Carrots in the future? Strauss comments, "We're committed to expanding the brand and concept as part of a long range plan that will include additional store openings."

Crazy Carrot was purchased by Jamba Juice in October of 1999.

Jamba Juice
San Francisco, California

Based in California, Juice Club opened its first store in April, 1990, in San Luis Obispo California by Kirk Perron, CEO and founder of the company. Kirk had worked for Safeway and Vons grocery stores prior to opening the first Juice Club.

An avid bicyclist, Kirk often craved a quick, healthy, portable meal after his long rides. Since there was not a place to get such a thing in his neighborhood, he'd return home to juice fresh fruits and vegetables or blend smoothies. Realizing that he probably wasn't alone in his thirst for a healthy alternative to fast food, he came up with the idea for Juice Club. After carefully planning the menu, architecture, and operational procedures, he opened the first store. Almost immediately, Juice Club filled a void in the community by giving people a place they could gather and feel good about what they ate. Juice Club began to expand.

By 1993, Juice Club opened two additional stores, and by 1994, it nearly quadrupled its size with 11 stores in operation. In July 1995, the company relocated its home office to San Francisco and introduced its new name and store concept: Jamba Juice.

The company began expansion efforts by offering franchises; however, in 1994, they ceased this practice and began their four-year goal of opening 130 company owned stores in California. Money was needed to finance the company's growth.

The firm received a huge influx of venture capital in the fall of 1994. Major contributors included Technology Venture Investors (TVI) and Benchmark Capital, who are both from Menlo Park, California. Three million came from TVI and an investment group led by chairman and CEO of Starbucks, Howard Schultz. Shortly after, the company received an additional 63 million in investment capital from various groups.

With several prominent venture capital groups, including Technology Venture Investors in Menlo Park, Trinity Ventures in San Mateo and San Francisco's Rosewood Capital, it is evident that Jamba Juice was poised for rapid expansion.

Jamba Juice was named "Hot New Concept" by Nation's Restaurant News in May 1998. This is recognition of innovation and prestige.

In February, 1999, the company announced it had agreed to acquire the Salt Lake City-based Zuka Juice in a straight stock deal.

According to Zuka Juice Founder and CEO Dave Duffin, Zuka Juice will retain its name in Salt Lake City, where the company was founded in 1995 and commands exceptional brand awareness. Duffin is now a board member for Jamba Juice Company.

Juice it Up!
Irvine, California

Based in Irvine California, Juice it Up! opened their first store in Brea California in March 1995 with the primary efforts of principles Larry Sidoti, and president, Greg Vujnov.

Following the success of a trailer operation, which is located on the campus of California State University at Fullerton, they opened their Chino store in Spring 1995.

The company places high standards for the quality of its products and places high valuation on the employees that operate the company stores.

The major turning point for the firm's business success: "The success of our first three stores: Brea, Chino and California State University, Fullerton, gave us a strong foundation to build upon."

Regarding the current and future of the Juice and Smoothie Business: Larry Sidoti states, " This industry today is still very much in its infant stages overall. The industry continues to grow and experience greater popularity. The product definitely is filling a niche and as [customer] awareness continues to grow, sales will continue to rise. I strongly believe those chains that are smart and controlled in their growth plans will emerge as the leaders... Juice Bars have created a market niche geared towards a healthier lifestyle. The industry has the potential to experience explosive growth in the coming years."

In July 1998 the company started offering franchise opportunities as a way to expand growth. The primary reasons are control and cost savings, according to Larry Sidoti.

"We do not have to absorb the labor overhead when a store is franchised. Labor is expensive with the advent of recent minimum wage increases.

In the Spring of 1999, the company completed a merger with Blue Sky Juice Company, which was a licensee of Juice it Up! from the eastern U.S.

Juice Stop

California Juice Stop
Mission Viejo, California

Juice Stop International: Juice Kitchen
Inglewood, Colorado

As of September, 1997, Juice Stop has operated as two separate entities: California Juice Stop Corporation, located in Mission Viejo (responsible for the state of California), and Juice Stop International Corporation (responsible for the remainder of the United States), which is located in Colorado.

The firm opened their first store in Lake Forest, California, in December 1993. The operation was overseen by T.J. Humphreys, founding partner. Humphreys collaborated with family member and concept developer, Susan Jespersen, to open their first outlet in Lake Forest in December, 1993.

The company's goal is to "help people lead healthier lives, and more active lifestyles, by providing nutritious products that are in tune with today's tastes and consumer trends."

The company decided on a franchise strategy early on in order to grow quickly, support expansion, and establish market share.

The company split in 1997. Juice Stop International was formed with its main office in Colorado. California Juice Stop remained in California under the watchful eyes of Susan Jesperson, president and Robert Johnson, vice president.

In November 1998 Juice Stop International announced that it had reorganized. The company also announced that it had hired a new management team. William Glennie, current president, announced that the company basically was starved for capital at the time and needed a more strategic approach to operations. William Glennie has over 10 years of franchise retail food service expertise with eight years of senior level sales and management in the specialty food industry for such well known companies as Pretzelmaker, Inc. and Mrs. Field's Cookies.

After closing several stores as part of the reorganization, Juice Stop International evolved into *Juice Kitchen*, which will oversee existing Juice Stop International franchisees.

Both California Juice Stop and Juice Kitchen remain viable players in the juice and smoothie industry today.

The best tasting smoothie on the planet!

Planet Smoothie

Atlanta, Georgia

After 6 months of detailed planning, Martin Sprock and Robert Brand opened their first smoothie store in Atlanta, Georgia. It was August, 1995, and Sprock, CEO, and Brand, current Operations Manager, along with a handful of investors, envisioned a basic mission that was to "Have fun building the best and largest smoothie company on the planet." Within a year, the company had many more locations.

By the end of 1996, the company was operating 10 stores; by the end of 1997, there were 25 stores in operation. The firm plans 100 stores by the end of 1998; 250 stores by the end of 1999, and 500 stores by the year 2000.

Planet Smoothie's growth plans include a combination of license and franchise (starting in January, 1998) agreements in conjunction with company owned stores. They are negotiating a global strategy as evidenced by the current ongoing negotiations to open stores in railway stations in the United Kingdom. The company exemplifies a diverse management team.

As of May 1999, the company has ceased licensing. The company has bought back most of its licensee locations and is now offering franchise deals.

With 65 domestic locations, the company's strategy is to dominate the eastern part of the U.S. Market.
"The primary constraint to growth", Sprock contends, "is real estate."

Martin Sprock's background is in real estate, restaurants, and bars. He currently has an 11unit restaurant chain in the Southeast. The remainder of the 10 partners bring to the table such diverse backgrounds as: CPA, restaurant management, real estate, law, banking, and marketing.

According to Sprock, the major turning point in the company's business success was, "having enough stores to support company employee wages and overhead."

Robeks Juice
Manhattan Beach, California

The history of Robeks Juice dates back to the early 1980's when its founder, David Robertson, began making smoothies as part of his exercise and weight loss regimen while he was a student at U.C. San Diego. After graduating from Harvard Business School in the early 1990's, David returned to Southern California to find smoothie bars popping up throughout the region. David decided to open his own smoothie bar featuring premium, made-to-order smoothies and fresh-squeezed juices. The name Robeks is a marriage of David's nickname, Robe, and the word aerobics.

In 1996, the first Robeks Juice opened in Westchester, California, and quickly developed a reputation for great tasting smoothies and fresh squeezed juices. During the next three years, Robeks opened an additional eighteen stores and expanded its product offering to include nutritious foccacia and wrap-style sandwiches, soups, baked goods, and a broad selection of health-related books and home juicing equipment. Robeks continued to focus solely on products that were consistent with its healthy lifestyle positioning.

Robeks developed their Nutribek™ line of nutritional boosts. These proprietary supplements, which may be added to a smoothie or juice to address a customer's specific nutritional needs, became so popular that they are now sold on a retail basis for home use.

As the juice & smoothie bar industry continues to evolve, Robeks believes that customers will increasingly differentiate between smoothie bar operators and begin to develop brand loyalty. Robeks Juice is well positioned to build on its reputation for superior product quality, nutritional value, and customer service.

Over the few years, Robeks plans to open 125 corporate-owned stores in California, and implement an area development and licensing program to develop an additional 250 stores in markets outside California. In order to support its aggressive expansion plans, Robeks has recruited a senior management team with extensive experience in high growth retail concepts.

Smoothie King

Kenner, Louisiana

Based in Louisiana, Smoothie King was started in 1987 by Stephen and Cynthia Kuhnau. In 1989, the company sold their first franchise. They currently offer single unit franchises and multi-unit development agreements. Ask Stephen Kuhnau if he ever dreamed he'd be known as the "Smoothie King" and you'll get a resounding, "No!". This, despite his commitment to a healthy lifestyle and passion about spreading the word that good nutrition improves health.

Stephen Kuhnau claims that it was destiny that led him to where he is today, and that his success could not have come without the health struggles he faced as a youth. "As I look back on all the challenges and opportunities that I was exposed to in my life," he says, "I realize that they were all pointing me in this direction."

As a teenager in the early 60's, trips to doctors and allergists brought him no relief and left him frustrated and determined to find an alternative cure for his ailments. Working at a local Hopper's Drive-in, he began experimenting with the many ingredients he had at his disposal - bananas, pineapples, strawberries and more. However, there was a twist to his shakes. Knowing that he needed additional proteins, vitamins and minerals to combat his low blood sugar and to build his immune system, Kuhnau began adding some nutritional formulas. In addition, believing he had an allergy to whole milk, he concocted his drinks without the standard milk ingredients. The result were shakes that tasted delicious, boosted his energy, and elevated his blood sugar without requiring him to consume large amounts.

Time passed and Kuhnau found himself in the Army Reserves stationed at a fort in Texas where he worked as a nurse for the Brooks Burn Center. The position gave him plenty of opportunities to learn about nutrition and the effect of diet on body tissue. He followed his stint in the service with a position as a leasing executive at Ford Motor Co. in Dearborn, Michigan. When Ford opened a satellite leasing office in New Orleans, the company asked Kuhnau to be in charge.

Throughout his successful years with Ford, Kuhnau continued to study nutrition and experiment with protein drinks. When he decided to go into business for himself, he realized it was natural for him to combine his business skills with his passion for nutrition. In 1973, he mortgaged his home and opened Town and Country Berth Foods in Kenner, Louisiana, where he offered smoothies on the side for 99 cents.

Twelve years later, Kuhnau met and hired Cindy Zimmer, who had worked for another local health food store for many years. Cindy's interest in nutrition stemmed from her desire to improve the health of her son, who had allergies similar to Stephen's. Working together, they realized they not only shared a passion for natural foods and healthy living, they also shared a passion for each other. A few years later, they were married.

It was Cindy who had a hunch that Stephen's hallmark smoothies - formulated on the spot by blending real fruits and fruit juices with an impressive array of wholesome nutrients that Kuhnau researched and tasted, along with a nutritional product store - had the potential to be more than a sideline. In 1989, they opened their first Smoothie King franchise on Baronne Street in New Orleans. Three other stores soon followed. Over the years, the steady stream of franchises have helped the company grow.

Smoothies may have brought Kuhnau great wealth, but the richest reward, he says, comes from the satisfaction he gets when customers become converted to maintaining a healthy lifestyle with the help of his smoothies and nutritional products. "When customers tell me they have more energy and feel better, " he says, "it's the best feeling in the world."

Smoothie Procedures

Procedures

Smoothies! The Original Smoothie Book
Recipes From The Pro's

The Basics

Smoothies consist of: Fruit juice, crushed ice, and/or ice-milk/nonfat frozen yogurt. Then, add fresh and/or frozen fruit (IQF). If desired, you can add vitamin supplements. We call these "Mix-ins".

Ice Milk

Ice milk is a dessert product, which is produced to be like ice cream but without all the fat. If you cannot find it at your local grocer, you can use nonfat frozen yogurt.

Nonfat Frozen Yogurt

Frozen yogurt is basically like ice milk, except it has yogurt culture added. Sometimes the yogurt culture, depending how much is used, can give a smoothie a sour taste. There are several brands that are good: Ralph's grocery store brand frozen yogurt is good if you plan to make your smoothies at home.

Crushed Ice

Most restaurants have large commercial ice machines that produce crushed ice for their needs. However, consumer units are available for a modest price. The easiest way to make your crushed ice at home is to put several ice cubes in a freezer storage bag and crush it with a tenderizing mallet. We will talk more about this later in "Basic Procedures".

Fruit

A core element of a smoothie is the fruit that it contains. Fresh fruit is the most desirable; however, when fruit is out of season IQF, which stands for *individually quick-frozen*, will work fine. You can purchase IQF fruit in the frozen produce section of your local market.

Juice

Juice can be purchased at your local grocery store or health food store. We recommend that you use frozen concentrate or bottled juice. We have provided recipes based around frozen concentrates produced by "Chiquita" and "Dole". This should help get you started, and keep your shopping to a minimum.

Juice Blends and Juice Concentrates

Some juices contain just what the label says on the container, such as raspberry, boysenberry, or apple. However, others are made with a variety of ingredients in order to get a specific flavor with the final goal being a sweet and tart satisfying taste.

Industry sources say that the juices of many fruits are too sour and acidic to taste good by themselves. In many instances juice concentrates are used for adding sweetening and to balance the tartness of the fruit juice. Furthermore, these blends are created to bring out the flavors of other fruit juice tastes in the "blend".

Other ingredients and natural flavors are often added to the formula to achieve the ideal juice blend or juice concentrate. Concentrates are used because, in general, fruits are needed when they are out of season. Brazil ships juice concentrates and many tropical fruits, all over the world. This is the only economically feasible way to achieve economies of scale. Juice concentrates are what allow juice and smoothie bar owners to offer a product at a fair price and still maintain a profit.

White grape juice is used to sweeten, intensify, and level out the flavor of many fruit juices and concentrates. White grape juice is often used in juice concentrate blends as a sweetener in order to retain a legal juice specification under FDA regulations. Although white grape juice is less expensive than some other juices, it is still much more expensive than corn syrup. Corn syrup is the sweetener of choice in mass-market juices and has little nutritional value.

White grape juice provides a variety vitamins, including A, C and E.

Some manufacturers have been known to process white grape juice to remove the flavor and nutrients. The result is basically sugar water. These manufacturers may make the claim that their product is 100 percent juice. However, the product may no longer qualify as a fruit juice under FDA regulations. This processed juice allows these manufacturers to reduce costs by using poor quality, low-cost fruit juice concentrates as sweeteners.

Mass-market juice products, in general, contain refined sugars, preservatives, and other chemically derived substances, yet still qualify as natural flavors according to FDA definitions.

Many juice concentrate suppliers will promote their products as natural. However, a closer look will reveal that the products are really sweetened with refined sugar, or have other legally approved "natural" ingredients. The basic premise is, "If it tastes good, it must be good for you." "Natural flavors" depict ingredients that provide intensification to the main flavors in fruit juices and fruit juice concentrates. Natural flavors can increase the impression of the fruit juice integrity and overall taste by enhancing what is already there, just like spices bring out the tastes in other foods. However, the term "natural flavors" can mean something else entirely. Therefore, use discretion when choosing your smoothie ingredients.

Fresh Juicing Tips

Juicing Equipment

Centrifugal Juice Machines

Centrifugal juice machines, the most popular for commercial juice bar operations, cut fruit and vegetables into very small pieces and separate the juice from the pulp via a high speed spinning strainer-basket. As the produce is cut, it is thrown up against the sides of the basket where the juice goes down a channel into a container. The pulp goes into another channel. The process is similar to the spin cycle on your washing machine when the tub spins to remove excess water from your clothes.

Most commercial juice machines have a pulp extractor coupler that can have a pipe attached to it in order to direct the pulp into a waste container. These types of juice machines are best for hard fruits and vegetables like carrots, apples, pears, and beets, etc.

Press Juice Machines

Press juice machines do not masticate (chop and cut) the produce. The juice is removed through pressure, which is built-up from an auger screw. This process is similar to how a meat grinder works. When you put meat into a meat grinder, an auger screw rotates when you turn the crank. This builds up pressure as the meat is compressed against the "strainer". These types of juice machines are best suited for soft produce like sprout grass and leaf vegetables. This is the only known type of juicer, which will remove wheat grass juice effectively.

Many citrus juice machines use a press process to remove juice. The most popular is a spindle juice machine, whereby a half piece of citrus is held by hand and pressed against a rotating spindle. This process is simple, and it is efficient.

Masticating Juice Machines

Masticating (means to chop/mash into small pieces) juice machines first chop the produce; then, pushes the pulp into a tube, via a screw auger, where the pulp is pressed tightly against a strainer screen to remove the juice. The process is a combination of the centrifugal and the press process, in that the produce is first chopped, then pressed.
Though not as efficient as a centrifugal juice machine, masticating juicers can be used as grinders for nuts and seeds. They also work well for both soft and hard produce, with the exception of wheat grass.

Ingredients

Fruit

IQF stands for *individually quick-frozen*, and is a term used for frozen produce. You can buy the frozen berries in the frozen food section of the grocery store. These are the same berries used for baking pies at home. These products are a popular choice because not all fruits are available year round. However, use seasonal fruit when it is available.

Banana

This fruit adds to the smoothness of a smoothie and adds to its overall consistency. It's the *salt and pepper* of the smoothie world. If you use too much the banana, will overpower the taste of a smoothie by not allowing the subtle taste of the other ingredients to come through. Try to use bananas that have no green on the peel and exhibit no more than a few brown spots. Be aware that as bananas ripen, they generally get stronger in taste.

Note that many recipes in this book call for banana. Unless otherwise specified, "x inch piece banana", means the amount that you cut off of a medium banana.

Coconut

Use unsweetened shredded coconut if you can find it.
However, if this is hard to find at the local grocery store, use
the sweetened kind. It will work just fine.

Bonus Mix-ins

Bonus Mix-ins are basically vitamin supplements that are put into smoothies to enhance the overall appeal and to add nutrients to the drink. They are popular because people can customize their drink to their nutritional needs. You can add whatever you wish. Keep in mind that some of these supplements will change the taste. One rounded teaspoon provides a single serving portion.

We have included a list of popular vitamin mix-in supplements here:

Bee Pollen

One of the most popular supplements, pollen is a fine powder-like material produced by the anthers of flowering plants and gathered by the bee. This "male" pollen contains over 8-complex vitamins, including: Vitamin C, amino acids, polyunsaturated fatty acids, enzymes, carotene, calcium, copper iron, magnesium, potassium, manganese, sodium, and protein.

Pollen has longtime been considered a superior supplement and contains every substance needed to maintain life. Health claims have been made about bee pollen, such as increased sexual stamina, to slowing down the aging process. *Caution: People with allergies to pollens may have a reaction to bee pollen.* Bee Pollen will slightly change the taste of a smoothie.

Brewer's Yeast

Brewer's yeast is grown from hops and is known as nutritional yeast. Originally a byproduct of the beer brewing process, brewer's yeast has a nut-like flavor, which is favorite supplement for protein and breakfast drinks. Brewer's yeast is rich in many nutrients, such as the B-vitamins (except for B12), chromium, sixteen amino acids, fourteen or more minerals, seventeen vitamins (except A, C, and E). Brewer's yeast has been reported to increase energy and help in sugar metabolism in the body. People have used this as an aid for eczema, heart disorders, nervousness, gout and fatigue. This supplement has a very strong taste and will change the taste of any smoothie.

Lecithin

Most Lecithin is derived from soybeans. It is composed of the 8 essential vitamins. Lecithin is a fatty substance. However, it acts as an emulsifying agent to prevent the accumulation of fat and cholesterol. It helps assimilate the fat-soluble vitamins A, D, K, and F. It is reported to promote energy, protect against cardiovascular disease, increase brain function, and help the absorption of vitamin A by the intestine.

Oat and Rice Bran

Is the outer-most portion of the seed kernel. It is the shell that protects the seed. When this shell is removed by processing the seed, it is called bran. Oat and rice bran are excellent sources of water-soluble fiber and help to lower blood serum cholesterol levels. It also aids in moving of food quickly through the digestive tract, thereby helping to prevent constipation.

Wheat Germ

Wheat germ is the kernel, or "heart", of the wheat berry. It is extremely high in vitamin E, as well as the B vitamin family. Nutritionally, it is the richest part of the wheat berry. The best part is that wheat germ is approximately 29% complete protein, making it an excellent source of protein for the vegetarian. Originally a foodstuff for animals, this supplement has gradually found its way into homes in recent years.

Blue-green algae

Is recognized the world over. It is considered by many as an immediate food resource. It thrives in hot sunny climates and in alkaline waters around the world. It represents a breakthrough in the production of food, producing twenty times the amount of protein as that of soybeans on an equal land area. Blue-green algae contains concentrations of many nutrients. It has high amounts of vegetable protein and is one of the best sources of vitamins, minerals, and amino acids in a whole food. It is rich in beta-carotene and B12, too. This supplement will slightly change the taste of a smoothie.

Wheat Bran

Comes from the outer layers of the wheatberry. Wheat bran is known to help food move through quickly through the digestive tract. And therefore, it is known to help prevent constipation. The National Cancer Institute recommends that we consume approximately 30 grams of fiber a day. Wheat Bran is an easy way to obtain this requirement.

Ginseng

This supplement is used throughout the Orient as a tonic for general weakness and extra energy. It has been said that the American Indians were familiar with ginseng. They used it for stomach and bronchial disorders, asthma, and neck pain. Scientists claim that the ginseng root stimulates both physical and mental activity, and has been said to offer a positive effect on the sex glands. It is currently being used for fatigue by sparring glycogen utilization in muscle, which increases the use of fatty acids as an energy source. It is also used to enhance athletic performances, increase longevity, detoxify, and normalize the entire system. This supplement will slightly change the taste of a smoothie.

Protein Powders

There are many protein powders currently on the market. Most are soy based with different additives, vitamins and enzymes that help differentiate the particular brand in the market place. Pound-for-pound, these powders exhibit more protein than beef, and are an excellent source for increasing the general protein requirements of the body.

Calcium

Calcium is the most important mineral in the body. It is essential for healthy blood, eases insomnia, and helps regulate the heartbeat. It is also important for the sound formation of bones.

There are many, many more popular vitamin mix-ins. Vitamin supplements are in vogue one day and out the next. Just remember that you can put just about any supplement you choose in your smoothie.

Source: Diet for Health

Popular Produce

Carrots

In his book *The Juicing Book*, Stephen Blauer purports carrot juice "...as the King of all juices...extremely high in pro-vitamin A, which the body converts to vitamin A. Carrot juice also contains the vitamins B, C, D, E, and K...as an overall tonic and rejuvenator, carrot juice can't be beat!"

Juicing carrots have the same nutritional value as table carrots. They provide the same amount of juice. They are, well, ugly; hence, they cost less. In contrast table carrots are usually nice and straight; and look good on a plate next to the peas and mashed potatoes.

You can get juicing carrots from your local produce supplier. If they do not have them in stock, simply order them. Juicing carrots generally come in 25 to 50 pound sacks.

Prep your carrots as soon as you get them. Empty them into your kitchen sink. Run cold water over the stock and inspect for damaged or spoiled carrots. Scrub each carrot with a bristle brush in order to remove any dirt or residue enzyme inhibitor; then, cut off the top of each carrot where mold and debris have collected. When you have completed this, rinse the carrots with cold water. Finally, put all the carrots in a large container, or sink, and cover all the carrots with cold water. Add ice to the water and soak them at least 12 hours before juicing them. This method will keep your carrots crisp and will provide a much better juice yield because the carrots will absorb water while they are soaking.

Do not refrigerate carrots for long periods of time, as this has a tendency to dry them out. Remember to pre-soak in order to get the best juice yield. Store carrot juice no longer than 36 hours. It has a very short self-life, usually less than 48 hours.

Oranges

In his classic book, *Back to Eden*, Jethro Kloss exploits the benefits of the orange. "The orange is one of nature's finest gifts to man. Orange juice, rich in enzymes, in a most delicious and attractive form, is ready for immediate absorption and utilization by the body. The amount of food value contained in a single large orange is about equivalent to that found in slice of wheat bread. But, orange juice differs from bread in that it needs no digestion, while bread, before it can be used, must undergo digestion for several hours. A glass of orange juice is equivalent to a glass of milk."

Valencia oranges are in season February to November. They are sweet, juicy, and have some seeds. They are excellent for juice and/or eating. Valencia oranges are grown in California and Arizona. They begin to turn golden in the winter months, long before they are ripe. Even though they may look ripe, it takes months of tree ripening before these oranges are ready to pick. However, an unusual phenomenon of nature happens.

As the Valencia orange hangs on the tree during the warm days of summer, the orange-colored oranges begin to turn green again beginning at the stem end. Experts call this "regreening". They blame it on warm ground temperatures, which cause the chlorophyll to return to the surface of the skin. The longer the Valencia's remain on the tree, the greener they become. So, actually, instead of being unripe, these green-tinged oranges are fully ripe and ready for consumption.

In contrast, Navel oranges, are in season November through May. They are sweet and juicy, with only an occasional seed. These oranges are easy to peel and excellent for eating. Their color is more consistent with the "orange" color we are all accustomed to.

There are principally two grades of oranges: premium and choice grade. The premium grade represents the highest grade and does not exhibit any imperfections, interior or exterior. This fruit sells for a higher price than choice grade, and is really more conducive to "table", or eating oranges. It is not necessary to use premium grade for juicing purposes; choice grade will work fine.

Keep your fresh Valencia juicing oranges in a cool, well-ventilated area. The best temperature range for citrus storage is 45 to 48 degrees F.

Basic Procedure

Use this basic procedure for all of the recipes unless otherwise noted.

Required equipment

- High-speed Food/Drink blender
- Ice-cream scoop
- Measuring cup
- Tenderizing mallet (to crush ice)
- Large zip-lock freezer bag
- Medium size mixing bowl
- Long standard 8 inch metal soda spoon

Blenders

The most important piece of equipment is your high-speed blender. There are dozens of these machines on the market. Choose a blender based on its container capacity and features. Is the container large enough to meet your needs? A simple two-speed blender is fine for mixing smoothies. You can purchase a blender at any discount store.

High-speed blenders will chop ice cubes just fine; however, this dulls the blender blades quickly and shortens the life of your blender. Here is a better way to crush your ice.

Ice Procedures

The most difficult part of making a smoothie is crushing the ice.

Put several ice cubes into the large zip-lock freezer bag. Zip the bag leaving the trailing end open about a 1/2 inch. This will allow air to escape and will prevent the bag from breaking when you strike it.

Fold a dishtowel over the freezer bag and place the configuration on a breadboard or a slicing table. The dishtowel will help dampen the blows from the mallet and prevent the bag from splitting open.

Begin to crush the ice by gently tapping the dishtowel. It is not necessary to hit the bag really hard. Move the mallet in a circular motion until you see that all the lumps of ice are split and broken. Adjust the bag every so often if necessary; continue to "tap-down" the ice. It is not necessary to crush the ice until it is as uniform as an ice-crushing machine would make it. The goal is to get it to a consistency so that you can measure it accurately. Of course, the amount of ice you crush is dependent on how many smoothies you plan to make.

You do not want to crush ice once you start making smoothies. The process will only slow you down. So, be sure you fill your mixing bowl(s) accordingly.

Initially crushed ice is dry; it will not have any water on it. As it melts, water forms at the bottom of the container or tub it is being stored in. If you try to refreeze the crushed ice by scooping it up and putting it into a freezer, you will be putting "wet" ice into the freezer. Within 30 minutes you will have a solid block of ice!

Mixing

Part of the appeal of a smoothie is to see a smoothie created right before your eyes. That's one of the appeals of a juice and smoothie bar - *ShowTime!*

- **First measure the fruit juice in the blender.** This is easy because most blender containers have convenient hash marks on them to aid in measuring.

- **Add in ice milk or frozen yogurt.** Gently push down with ice cream scoop so that mixture hits the blender blades.

- **Add desired vitamin supplements and crushed ice** (in that order). Gently push down again with the ball of the ice-cream scoop.

- **Finally, add in the fresh/frozen fruit.** Blend at high-speed until mixture is smooth and creamy.

Blender Cavitation

Many home blenders and even commercial blenders may have trouble mixing a smoothie. Many times the bottom half of the smoothie in a blender container will mix very well; however, the top half will not get mixed because of an air pocket (cavitation), or the ice and fruit is not getting "pulled" to the bottom of the container by the blender blades. These air pockets can cause the blender motor to whine out of control. This can happen because the solid parts of the smoothie are not hitting the blender blades properly. The solution is to shut off the blender. Pick up the container and give it a few jerks with a downward stopping motion. This will "reseat" the mixture. Place the container back on the spindle and continue.

Tip: Never put vitamin mix-in powder supplements on the very top of the mixture because these will "explode" into the lid of the blender, thereby making it difficult to wash later.

<u>Caution:</u> Never remove the lid of a blender while the machine is running. This can be extremely dangerous!

Smoothie
Recipes

Berry-Berry Cool

A boysenberry-blueberry blend that is rich, fruity, and oh yes! Berrrry cool!

6 ounces of boysenberry juice
2 ounces of raspberry juice
2 frozen boysenberries
6 frozen blueberries
1 cup nonfat frozen vanilla yogurt
1 1/4 cup crushed ice

Nutritional Information: Serving size approx. 20 ounces
Calories 306
Total fat 0g
Saturated fat 0g
Cholesterol 0mg
Sodium 15mg
Total Carbohydrates 68g
Dietary fiber 0.47g
Protein 3g

Yo Mango Mania

This mango, pineapple mingle is mighty movin'.

7 ounces of mango juice
1 ounce of pineapple juice
1 cup nonfat frozen vanilla yogurt
1 1/4 cup crushed ice

Nutritional Information: Serving size approx. 20 ounces
Calories 250
Total fat 0g
Saturated fat 0g
Cholesterol 0mg
Sodium 20mg
Total Carbohydrates 69g
Dietary fiber 0.47g
Protein 3g

Down-Beat

Orange and cranberry juice create a duo taste; the rhythm section is slammin' with raspberry and blueberry.

6 ounces of orange juice
2 ounces of cranberry juice
3 frozen raspberries
6 frozen blueberries
1 cup nonfat frozen vanilla yogurt
1 1/4 cup crushed ice

Nutritional Information: Serving size approx. 20 ounces
Calories 307
Total fat 0g
Saturated fat 0g
Cholesterol 0mg
Sodium 3mg
Total Carbohydrates 72g
Dietary fiber 0.48g
Protein 4.6g

Rembrandt — *Very Popular*

Apple juice, strawberry juice, and banana paint the perfect profile.

7 ounces of strawberry juice
1 ounce of apple juice
1 inch piece banana
1 cup nonfat frozen vanilla yogurt
1 1/4 cup crushed ice

Nutritional Information: Serving size approx. 20 ounces
Calories 295
Total fat 0.15g
Saturated fat 0.03g
Cholesterol 0mg
Sodium 20mg
Total Carbohydrates 69g
Dietary fiber 0.47g
Protein 3g

Goophy Guava

A guava, orange, and pineapple integration that is island tropicana.

7 ounces of guava juice
1/2 ounce of pineapple juice
1/2 ounce of orange juice
1 cup nonfat frozen vanilla yogurt
1 1/4 cup crushed ice

Nutritional Information: Serving size approx. 20 ounces
Calories 280
Total fat 0g
Saturated fat 0g
Cholesterol 0mg
Sodium 0.96mg
Total Carbohydrates 63g
Dietary fiber 2g
Protein 2.8g

1-4-5 Blues

Apple juice, blueberries, and banana jazz up this trio.

4 ounces of apple juice
4 ounces of raspberry juice
6 blueberries fresh or frozen
1 inch piece banana
1 cup nonfat frozen vanilla yogurt
1 1/4 cup crushed ice

Nutritional Information: Serving size approx. 20 ounces
Calories 297
Total fat 0g
Saturated fat 0g
Cholesterol 0mg
Sodium 13.6mg
Total Carbohydrates 70g
Dietary fiber 0.2g
Protein 2.98g

Rainbow Symphony

A palette of fruit and juices! This frosty cocktail includes strawberries, blueberries, bananas, peaches, raspberries, boysenberries, and coconut.

4 ounces of raspberry juice
1 ounce of boysenberry juice
1 ounce peach juice
2 ounce strawberry juice
6 blueberries
1 strawberry
2 raspberries
1 boysenberry
1/8 slice of peach
2 cherries
1 inch piece banana
1 tablespoon shredded coconut
1 cup nonfat frozen vanilla yogurt
3/4 cup crushed ice

Nutritional Information: Serving size approx. 20 ounces
Calories 307
Total fat 0.81g
Saturated fat 0.62g
Cholesterol 0mg
Sodium 15.4mg
Total Carbohydrates 70.7g
Dietary fiber 0.72g
Protein 3.19g

Picasso – *Very Popular*

Pineapple juice, peach, banana, and coconut fusion make this a modernistic treat.

6 ounces of pineapple juice
2 ounces of peach juice
1/8 slice of peach
1 inch piece banana
1 tablespoon of shredded coconut
1 cup nonfat frozen vanilla yogurt
1 1/4 cup crushed ice

Nutritional Information: Serving size approx. 20 ounces
Calories 306
Total fat 0.15g
Saturated fat 0.03g
Cholesterol 0mg
Sodium 2.1mg
Total Carbohydrates 74g
Dietary fiber 0.70g
Protein 3.49g

Rockin' Bowl

A fruit bowl of fruit flavors complement this cranberry juice, strawberry, and raspberry concoction.

4 ounces of raspberry juice
2 ounces of strawberry juice
2 ounces of cranberry juice
1 strawberry
3 raspberries
2 cherries
1 cup nonfat frozen vanilla yogurt
1 1/4 cup crushed ice

Nutritional Information: Serving size approx. 20 ounces
Calories 315
Total fat 0g
Saturated fat 0g
Cholesterol 0mg
Sodium 12.6mg
Total Carbohydrates 76g
Dietary fiber 0.56g
Protein 2.97g

All-In-One

This is the ultimate in raspberries, blueberries, boysenberries, strawberries, and banana. A *powershake* for the active person!

4 ounces of raspberry juice
2 ounces of strawberry juice
2 ounces of boysenberry juice
1 strawberry
2 boysenberries
6 blueberries
2 inch piece banana
1 cup nonfat frozen vanilla yogurt
1 1/4 cup crushed ice

Nutritional Information: Serving size approx. 20 ounces
Calories 316
Total fat 0.15g
Saturated fat 0.03g
Cholesterol 0mg
Sodium 10.4mg
Total Carbohydrates 73g
Dietary fiber 0.95g
Protein 3.19g

Peachy-Keen

This is the peach lover's delight. Made with peaches, peach juice, and fresh banana. This one is sure to please.

8 ounces of peach juice
1/8 slice of frozen peach
1 inch piece banana
1 cup nonfat frozen vanilla yogurt
1 1/4 cup crushed ice

Nutritional Information: Serving size approx. 20 ounces
Calories 290
Total fat 0g
Saturated fat 0g
Cholesterol 0mg
Sodium 0.96mg
Total Carbohydrates 69g
Dietary fiber 1.14g
Protein 2.84g

My-Ya-Papaya

A rich froth of delectable coconut, banana, and tropical papaya juice.

8 ounces of papaya juice
1 tablespoon shredded coconut
1 cup nonfat frozen vanilla yogurt
1 1/4 cup crushed ice

Nutritional Information: Serving size approx. 20 ounces
Calories 311
Total fat 0.81g
Saturated fat 0.62g
Cholesterol 0mg
Sodium 5mg
Total Carbohydrates 73g
Dietary fiber 0.17g
Protein 3g

The Workout

This smoothie is made to replenish. Made with mango and papaya juice. Ready to pump?

4 ounces of mango juice
4 ounces of papaya juice
1 tablespoon shredded coconut
1 cup nonfat frozen vanilla yogurt
1 1/4 cup crushed ice

Nutritional Information: Serving size approx. 20 ounces
Calories 310
Total fat 0.81g
Saturated fat 0.62g
Cholesterol 0mg
Sodium 5mg
Total Carbohydrates 73g
Dietary fiber 0.17g
Protein 3g

The smoothies in this section yield about 20 ounces.

Baby-Boomer

High in enzymes and a pineapple taste.

8 ounces of pineapple juice
1/2 cup of canned or fresh pineapple
2 inch piece banana
1 cup nonfat frozen vanilla yogurt
1 1/4 cup crushed ice

Generation X

The alternative taste.

4 ounces of orange juice
4 ounces of strawberry juice
3 medium strawberries
2 inch piece banana
1 cup nonfat frozen vanilla yogurt
1 1/4 cup crushed ice

Sunburst

The perfect mix of orange juice and red berries.

8 ounces of orange juice
2 medium strawberries
8 raspberries
4 cherries
2 inch piece banana
1 cup nonfat frozen vanilla yogurt
1 1/4 cup crushed ice

Et Cetera

Strawberry on strawberry.

8 ounces of strawberry juice
5 medium strawberries
2 inch piece banana
1 cup nonfat frozen vanilla yogurt
1 1/4 cup crushed ice

Mix-It-Up!

Cranberry and apple. Awesome taste.

6 ounces of cranberry juice
2 ounces of apple juice
1/2 cup fresh green Granny Smith apple
1 inch piece banana
1 cup nonfat frozen vanilla yogurt
1 1/4 cup crushed ice

Apples Galore

Apple lovers dream!

8 ounces of apple juice
1/2 fresh green Granny Smith apple
1 inch piece banana
1 cup nonfat frozen vanilla yogurt
1 1/4 cup crushed ice

Add cinnamon if desired.

Blue Bayou

Apple & blueberry combination.

7 ounces of apple juice
1 ounce boysenberry juice
1/8 of a fresh green Granny Smith apple
16 blueberries
1 inch piece banana
1 cup nonfat frozen vanilla yogurt
1 1/4 cup crushed ice

Too Cool

Orange-strawberry delight.

8 ounces of orange juice
4 strawberries
2 inch piece banana
1 cup nonfat frozen vanilla yogurt
1 1/4 cup crushed ice

Brava

A Latin ting with raspberry. Ooh-la-la!

6 ounces of raspberry juice
2 ounces of guava juice
6 blueberries
1 cup nonfat frozen vanilla yogurt
1 1/4 cup crushed ice

Quick Recipes

Here is a partial listing of frozen juice concentrate blends, which should be available at your local grocer. You can find them in the frozen juice section or in some cases already premixed in cartons. These recipes are called *"Quick Recipes"* because you can easily obtain the ingredients. The juice blends used in these recipes are offered by brand name companies and therefore are easy to get. You can start mixing smoothies right away. You can use generic store brand frozen juice concentrates, also; however, their flavor selection is usually much more limited than brand name products. Each of the smoothies in this section yields about 20 ounces. Here are the names of some brand name juice blends:

Dole Brand® Juice

- Pineapple Juice
- Orchard Peach
- Pineapple - Apple - Orange
- Country Raspberry
- Pineapple - Orange - Banana
- Mountain Cherry
- Mandarin Tangerine
- Pine-Orange-Guava

Chiquita Brand® Juice

- Calypso Breeze - Strawberry and kiwi blend
- Caribbean Splash - Pineapple, apple, and guava
- Tropical Paradise - Orange, Strawberry, and banana
- Raspberry Passion - Blend of six juices
- Cranberry Seabreeze - Cranberry juice

Dole Brand Recipes

Pineapple-Apple-Orange

---

8 ounces of Dole Brand Pineapple-Apple-Orange
2 strawberries
2 inch piece banana
1 cup nonfat frozen vanilla yogurt
1 1/4 cup crushed ice

Pineapple-Orange-Banana

---

8 ounces of Dole Brand Pineapple-Orange-Banana
1 strawberry
6 blueberries
1 inch piece banana
1 tablespoon of shredded coconut
1 cup nonfat frozen vanilla yogurt
1 1/4 cup crushed ice

Mandarin Tangerine

---

8 ounces of Dole Brand Mandarin Tangerine
1 inch piece banana
1 cup nonfat frozen vanilla yogurt
1 1/4 cup crushed ice

Tangy Nectarine

---

1 whole nectarine, pitted and peeled
6 ounces regular peach yogurt
1/2 cup Dole Brand Pine-Orange-Guava juice
1/2 cup lemonade

Chiquita Brand Recipes

Calypso Breeze

---

8 ounces of Chiquita Brand Calypso Breeze blend
2 strawberries
4 cherries
4 raspberries
1 inch piece banana
1 cup nonfat frozen vanilla yogurt
1 1/4 cup crushed ice

Caribbean Splash

---

8 ounces of Chiquita Brand Caribbean Splash
6 blueberries
3 boysenberries
1 inch piece banana
1 cup nonfat frozen vanilla yogurt
1 1/4 cup crushed ice

Tropical Paradise

---

8 ounces of Chiquita Brand Tropical Paradise
2 strawberries
2 inch piece banana
1 cup nonfat frozen vanilla yogurt
1 1/4 cup crushed ice

Creamy Smoothies

Use regular nonfat yogurt (not frozen nonfat yogurt) for the following recipes to make a smoother, more drinkable smoothie. Milk alternatives may be substituted for nonfat milk. *See the appendix for alternative milk recipes.* Drink yield in this section varies from drink to drink.

Coconut Apple Smoothie

1/2 cup apple juice
1 tablespoon shredded coconut
1/2 banana
1/4 teaspoon fresh ginger root, grated
1/2 cup crushed ice

Apricot Nectarine Smoothie

---

1 whole nectarine, seeded and peeled
1 whole apricot, pitted
1 cup regular nonfat vanilla yogurt
4 ounces lemon juice
1/2 cup crushed ice

Mango-Apricot Smoothie

---

6 ounces regular nonfat apricot-mango yogurt
1 cup lemonade
1/2 banana
2 whole apricots, pitted

Blueberry Smoothie

---

6 ounces regular blueberry yogurt
1 cup blueberries fresh or frozen
1 cup nonfat milk

Kiwi Strawberry

---

3 peeled kiwi
1 medium banana
3/4 cup pineapple juice
5 medium strawberries

Cantaloupe Smoothie

---

1 cup nonfat milk or milk alternative
1/2 cup orange juice
1 medium banana
1/2 cup cantaloupe
1/2 cup strawberries, fresh or frozen

Melon Smoothie

---

1 cup of regular peach nonfat yogurt
1 cup nonfat milk
1/2 cup cantaloupe
1/2 cup honey dew melon
1/2 cup crushed ice
4 strawberries

Nectarine Papaya Smoothie

---

1 cup lemonade
6 ounces regular peach nonfat yogurt
1 nectarine, seeded and peeled
1 cup papaya, seeded and peeled

Papaya Raspberry Smoothie

---

1 medium frozen banana
1/2 fresh papaya
10 raspberries
1/2 cup papaya juice

Carrot Smoothie

2 cups fresh carrot juice
1/2 cup apple juice
6 ounces nonfat vanilla frozen yogurt
1/2 banana

Classic Strawberry Smoothie

6 large strawberries
6 ounces regular nonfat strawberry yogurt
4 ounces lemonade

Strawberry Banana Smoothie

1 medium banana
6 large strawberries
1/2 cup nonfat milk
1/2 cup apple juice

Pistachio Smoothie

1 cup plain nonfat yogurt
1/2 cup raw pistachio nuts
1 medium ripe banana
1/4 cup nonfat milk
1/2 cup crushed ice

Peachy Apple Smoothie

10 ounces of apple juice
5 slices of peach
4 strawberries
1 medium banana
1/8 teaspoon cinnamon

Tofu Berry Smoothie

1 cup regular nonfat vanilla yogurt
1 cup nonfat milk
1 medium banana
3 inch cube of soft tofu
3/4 cup blueberries
5 medium strawberries

A Lot of Colada Smoothie

1 cup regular nonfat coconut yogurt
1/2 medium banana
1/2 cup pineapple
1 cup nonfat milk

Blackberry Smoothie

1/4 cup blueberries
1/4 cup blackberries
1 medium banana
1/2 cup apple juice
1/3 cup raspberry sherbet

Milk Based Smoothies

These smoothies are based around nonfat milk instead of fruit juice. If you wish, you can make these smoothies non-dairy by using any of the many milk dairy substitutes, which are now on the market. Use one cup of milk substitute to replace the nonfat frozen yogurt. Visit the dairy section of your local market to see the rice, oat and soy milk alternatives available. *See the appendix for alternative milk recipes.*

First Date

The classic date shake.

8 ounces nonfat milk
4 medium sweet dates
3 inch piece banana
1 cup nonfat frozen vanilla yogurt
1 1/4 cup crushed ice

Chocolate Fruit Smoothie

A Fruity Chocolate Taste.

8 ounces nonfat milk
4 boysenberries
6 raspberries
1 teaspoon carob powder
3 inch piece banana
1 cup nonfat frozen chocolate yogurt
1 1/4 cup crushed ice

Café De Chocolate

A coffee lover's delight.

8 ounces of cold regular or decaffeinated coffee
1 teaspoon carob powder
1 inch piece banana
1 cup nonfat frozen chocolate yogurt
1 1/4 cup crushed ice

Banana-Banana Smoothie

This is for the banana lover.

8 ounces nonfat milk
1 whole medium size banana
1 cup nonfat frozen vanilla yogurt
1 1/4 cup crushed ice

Cocoa De Carob

Chocolate taste with malt.

8 ounces nonfat milk
1 teaspoon carob powder
1 tablespoon of malted milk powder
1 cup nonfat frozen vanilla yogurt
1 1/4 cup crushed ice

Banana Chocolate Smoothie

A smooth chocolate banana taste.

8 ounces nonfat milk
1 teaspoon carob powder
3 inch piece banana
1 cup nonfat frozen vanilla yogurt
1 1/4 cup crushed ice

Peanut Butter Smoothie

---

8 ounces nonfat milk
1/4 cup crunchy or smooth peanut butter
1 cup nonfat frozen vanilla yogurt
1 1/4 cup crushed ice

Almond Butter Delight

---

8 ounces nonfat milk
1/4 cup almond butter
1 cup nonfat frozen vanilla yogurt
1 1/4 cup crushed ice

Cashew Butter Smoothie

---

8 ounces nonfat milk
1/4 cup cashew butter
1 inch piece banana
1 cup nonfat frozen vanilla yogurt
1 1/4 cup crushed ice

Holiday Smoothies

These smoothies can be served for special occasions and holidays.

Halloween/Thanksgiving Special

Real pumpkin! Serve with nutmeg sprinkles for a special treat!

8 ounces nonfat milk
1/2 - 3/4 cup canned, cooked pumpkin pie filling
1/4 teaspoon of pumpkin pie spice
1 cup nonfat frozen vanilla yogurt
1 1/4 cup crushed ice

December Holiday Smoothie

Made with real peppermint extract. Hang a candy cane on the side of the cup when you serve this holiday treat!

8 ounces nonfat milk
6 drops of peppermint extract
10 raspberries
1 cup nonfat frozen vanilla yogurt
1 1/4 cup crushed ice

Valentine Sweetheart Smoothie

---

8 ounces nonfat milk
4 medium strawberries
1 cup nonfat frozen vanilla yogurt
1 1/4 cup crushed ice

Saint Patrick's Day Green

Crown this smoothie with a sprig of peppermint!

8 ounces nonfat milk
6 drops of peppermint extract
8 drops of green food coloring
1 cup nonfat frozen vanilla yogurt
1 1/4 cup crushed ice

Recipes From Juice & Smoothie Companies

Crazy Carrot

Power Punch™

The Power Punch makes for a great after workout smoothie. Made with strawberries, blueberries, pineapple, cherries, bananas, nonfat frozen yogurt, freshly squeezed orange juice, protein, lecithin, and chromium picolinate.

8 ounces-freshly squeezed orange juice
1/2 banana
1 ounce blueberries
1 ounce strawberries
1 ounce pineapple
1 ounce cherries
3 ounces nonfat frozen yogurt
3 ounces ice
1 tsp. soy-based protein powder
1/2 tsp. lecithin
1/4 tsp. chromium picolinate

Nutritional Information: Serving size 664g
Calories 350
Total fat 2.5g
Saturated fat 0g
Cholesterol 0mgSodium 25mg Total Carbohydrates 78g
Dietary fiber 5g Sugars 66g Protein 8g

Mighty Mango™

Quite possibly the mightiest smoothie of them all, the **Mighty Mango** is just the right blend of mangos, strawberries, non-fat frozen yogurt, and freshly squeezed orange juice.

8 ounces freshly squeezed orange juice
2 ounces strawberries
2 ounces mango
3 ounces nonfat frozen yogurt
3 ounces ice

Nutritional Information: Serving size 583g
Calories 260
Total fat 0.5g
Saturated fat 0g
Cholesterol 0mg
Sodium 0mg
Total Carbohydrates 61g
Dietary fiber 2g
Sugars 54g
Protein 5g

Very Berry Blast™

A delightful blend of strawberries, raspberries, blackberries, and pure maple syrup make the Very Berry Blast very hard to resist.

8 ounces freshly squeezed orange juice
2 ounces strawberries
1 ounce blackberries
1 ounce raspberries
1 tablespoon pure maple syrup
3 ounces ice

Nutritional Information: Serving size 572g
Calories 220
Total fat 1g
Saturated fat 0g
Cholesterol 0mg
Sodium 5mg
Total Carbohydrates 51g
Dietary fiber5g
Sugars 43g
Protein 4g

Strawberry Serenade™

Strawberries, bananas, freshly squeezed orange juice, and pure honey, blended right before your eyes into a mouth-watering, eye-opening elixir.

8 ounces freshly squeezed orange juice
1/2 banana
3 ounces strawberries
1 tablespoon pure honey
3 ounces ice

Nutritional Information: Serving size 518g
Calories 210
Total fat 1g
Saturated fat 0g
Cholesterol 0mg
Sodium 0mg
Total Carbohydrates 52g
Dietary fiber 3g
Sugars 46g
Protein 3g

Berry Patch™

We challenge you to find another smoothie with more berries than the Berry Patch. The encore presentation includes strawberries, raspberries, blackberries, boysenberries, blueberries, raspberry sherbet, and apple juice.

8 ounces pure apple cider
1 ounce strawberries
1 ounce raspberries
1 ounce blackberries
1 ounce blueberries
1 ounce boysenberries
3 ounces raspberry sherbet
3 ounces ice

Nutritional Information: Serving size 662g
Calories 320
Total fat 1g
Saturated fat 0g
Cholesterol 0mg
Sodium 45mg
Total Carbohydrates 78g
Dietary fiber 6g
Sugars 63g
Protein 2g

Jamba Juice

The following recipes are from the private vault of Kirk Perron, CEO and founder of Jamba Juice. *"...With health and vitality!"*

Orange Ecstasy

---

12 ounces orange juice (squeezed or from concentrate)
2/3 cup frozen yogurt, vanilla nonfat
1 cup peaches, frozen unsweetened
1 whole banana, medium
1/2 cup ice, cubes or crushed

Nutritional Information: Serving size approx. 24 ounces
Calories 470
Total fat 1.5g
Saturated fat 0g
Cholesterol 0mg
Sodium 95mg
Total Carbohydrates 110g
Dietary fiber 7g
Sugars 100g
Protein 11g

Hawaiian Heaven

---

12 ounces pineapple juice, unsweetened canned or frozen
1 whole banana, medium
1 cup peaches, frozen unsweetened
1 tablespoon honey
1/2 cup mango, fresh diced or frozen unsweetened
1/2 cup ice, cubes or crushed

Nutritional Information: Serving size approx. 24 ounces
Calories 490
Total fat 1g
Saturated fat 0g
Cholesterol 0mg
Sodium 10mg
Total Carbohydrates 126g
Dietary fiber 9g
Sugars 113g
Protein 4g

Cranberry Cooler

---

12 ounces cranberry juice
2/3 cup orange sherbet
1 cup strawberries, frozen unsweetened
1/2 cup raspberries, frozen unsweetened
1/2 cup ice, cubes or crushed

Nutritional Information: Serving size approx. 24 ounces
Calories 480
Total fat 3.5g
Saturated fat 1.5g
Cholesterol 10mg
Sodium 70mg
Total Carbohydrates 115g
Dietary fiber 8g
Sugars 99g
Protein 3g

Juice It Up!

Note: 1 scoop equals 1 cup. One banana "chunk" equals 1/2 inch piece of banana.

Strawberry Wave

Ride the Surf! Strawberry Nectar with strawberries, banana, and yogurt.

10 ounces strawberry juice
1 scoop ice
1 banana chunk (1/2" piece)
2 scoops non-fat frozen vanilla yogurt
1 scoop strawberries

Nutritional Information
Serving size: 24 ounces
Calories 360
Fat grams 0.4gm
Carbohydrates 81gm
Protein 9gm

Big Berry Combo

Sing the Blues for this Juice it Up favorite!
Blueberries, raspberry sherbet, apple juice, banana, &
yogurt.

10 ounces apple juice
1 scoop ice
1 banana chunk
1 scoop non-fat frozen vanilla yogurt
1 scoop non-fat raspberry sherbet
1 scoop blueberries

Nutritional Information
Serving size: 24 ounces
Calories 400
Fat grams 1.0gm
Carbohydrates 93gm
Protein 7gm

Seabreeze Squeeze

Taste of California! Apple/cranberry blend, strawberries, raspberries, banana, orange sherbet, & yogurt.

5 ounces cranberry juice
5 ounces apple juice
1 scoop ice
1 banana chunk
1 scoop non-fat frozen yogurt
1 scoop non-fat orange sherbet
1/2 scoop strawberries
1/2 scoop raspberries

Nutritional Information
Serving size: 24 ounces
Calories 435
Fat grams 1.0gm
Carbohydrates 98gm
Protein 10gm

Raspberry Craze

Berry Overload! Cranberry/raspberry blend, Strawberries, raspberries, banana, and raspberry sherbet.

10 ounces raspberry juice
1 scoop ice
1 banana chunk
2 scoops non-fat raspberry sherbet
1/2 scoop strawberries,
1/2 scoop raspberries

Nutritional Information
Serving size: 24 ounces
Calories 470
Fat grams 2.0gm
Carbohydrates 112gm
Protein 3gm

Mango Mania

Maximum Mango! Mango juice, strawberries, peaches, banana, & yogurt.

10 ounces mango juice
1 scoop ice
1 banana chunk
2 scoops non-fat frozen yogurt
1/2 scoop peaches,
1/2 scoop strawberries

Nutritional Information
Serving size: 24 ounces
Calories 350
Fat grams 0.4gm
Carbohydrates 76gm
Protein 10gm

Juice Stop

Note: 1 scoop equals 1 cup.

Double Axle©

This orange-berry combination will send you soaring and twisting in the air.

10 ounces of orange juice
1 scoop of pineapple sherbet
5 slices of banana
1/2 scoop of strawberry
1/2 scoop of raspberry
1/2 scoop boysenberry
1/2 scoop ice

Nutritional Information: Serving size 24 oz.
Calories 346
Calories from fat 2%
Total fat 0.839g
Cholesterol 0.886mg
Total Carbohydrates 87.1g
Protein 2.21g

Off The Lip©

Drop into this strawberry, coconut, banana, and pineapple blend.

10 ounces of pineapple juice
1 scoop shredded coconut
1 tablespoon of honey
5 slices of banana
1 scoop strawberry
1/2 scoop ice

Nutritional Information: Serving size 24 oz.
Calories 347
Calories from fat 3%
Total fat 1.23g
Cholesterol 0mg
Total Carbohydrates 86.6g
Protein 1.97g

Tour de France©

This high energy apple, raspberry, blueberry, banana blend gets your wheels turning.

10 ounces apple juice
1 scoop non-fat frozen vanilla yogurt
1 scoop raspberry sherbet
5 slices banana
1 scoop blueberry
1/2 scoop ice

Nutritional Information: Serving size 24 oz.
Calories 322
Calories from fat 5%
Total fat 1.83g
Cholesterol 1.71mg
Total Carbohydrates 75.6g
Protein 5.35g

Half Pipe©

Skate into this sweet guava, peach, pineapple, and banana combination.

10 ounces of guava juice
1 scoop pineapple sherbet
10 slices of banana
1/2 scoop peaches
1/2 scoop ice

Nutritional Information: Serving size 24 oz.
Calories 325
Calories from fat 2%
Total fat 0.917g
Cholesterol 2.19mg
Total Carbohydrates 82.5g
Protein 2.12g

Side Out©

Pass, set, and spike your way to victory with this strawberry, apricot, peach, and banana sensation.

10 ounces of apricot juice
1/2 scoop orange sherbet
5 slices of banana
1 scoop strawberry
1 scoop peaches
1/2 scoop ice

Nutritional Information: Serving size 24 oz.
Calories 322
Calories from fat 2%
Total fat 0.752g
Cholesterol 0.886mg
Total Carbohydrates 81.5g
Protein 2.12g

Planet Smoothie

The best tasting smoothie on the planet!

Planet Smoothie

Planet Smoothie Smoothies are blended together with a proprietary mix of vitamins and supplements that are called Blasts. You can turn any Smoothie into a healthy meal that tastes great. Blasts are available at Planet Smoothie stores for you to take home and mix with your homemade smoothies or your favorite juice.

Billy Bob Banana™

---

2 1/2 bananas
1 tablespoon non-fat milk
1/4 teaspoon vanilla extract
1 tablespoon turbinado
16 ounces crushed ice

Calories 347
Protein 4.5g
Carbohydrates 87g

Last Mango™

---

4 ounces mango
3 ounces peaches
1/2 banana
4 ounces orange sherbet

Calories 355.4
Protein 3.3g
Carbohydrates 84.2g

Vinnie Del Rocco™

---

3 ounces blueberries
4 ounces raspberries
3 ounces strawberries
4 ounces orange sherbet

Calories 414
Protein 3.2g
Carbohydrates 99.5g

Robeks Juice

Nutribeks™ are Robeks special formulated nutritional boost supplements. You can purchase these at any Robeks retail outlets to put in the smoothies you make at home.

Venice Burner®

A fat burning blend of fresh-squeezed orange juice, peaches, bananas, pineapple sherbet, Trim•bek® Ginseng, and ice.

12 ounces orange juice
3 ounces peaches
3 ounces banana
6 ounces pineapple sherbet
3 ounces crushed ice
1/2 teaspoon ginseng
1 teaspoon Trim•bek® (Robeks all-natural fat burning supplement)

Nutritional Information: Serving size 24 oz.
Calories 409
Calories from fat 2.1g
Cholesterol 2% Total Carbohydrates 87.5g
Protein 6.3g Fiber 6.4g

Lemonator®

An energizing blend of fresh-squeezed lemonade, strawberries, pineapple sherbet, Ginseng, ice, and Vita•bek®

12 ounces fresh-squeezed lemonade
6 ounces strawberries
6 ounces pineapple sherbet
3 ounces crushed ice
1/2 teaspoon ginseng
1 teaspoon Vita•bek® (Robeks proprietary supplement containing 100% Daily Value of 20 essential vitamins and minerals)

Nutritional Information: Serving size 24 oz.
Calories 287
Calories from fat 1.3g
Cholesterol 2%
Total Carbohydrates 67.8g
Protein 2.1g
Fiber 3.4g

Pro Arobek®

Enhance your workout with this muscle building blend! Apple juice, bananas, raspberry sherbet, non-fat yogurt, creatine, soy protein, ice and Trim•bek®

12 ounces apple juice
6 ounces banana
3 ounces raspberry sherbet
3 ounces non-fat frozen vanilla yogurt
1/2 teaspoon creatine
1/2 teaspoon soy protein
3 ounces crushed ice
1 teaspoon Trim•bek® (Robeks all-natural fat burning supplement)

Nutritional Information: Serving size 24 oz.
Calories 422
Calories from fat 1.6g
Cholesterol 1%
Total Carbohydrates 98.5g
Protein 14.9g
Fiber 5.8g

South Pacific Squeeze®

A tropical blend of fresh-squeezed orange juice, pineapples, strawberries, bananas, pineapple sherbet, and ice.

10 ounces fresh-squeezed orange juice
3 ounces pineapple
2 ounces banana
3 ounces strawberries
6 ounces pineapple sherbet
3 ounces crushed ice

Nutritional Information: Serving size 24 oz.
Calories 390
Calories from fat 2.5g
Cholesterol 2%
Total Carbohydrates 88.2g
Protein 4.6g
Fiber 5.4g

Hummingbird®

Robeks signature smoothie!
Guava juice, mangos, strawberries, bananas, orange sherbet, and ice.

10 ounces guava juice
3 ounces mangos
3 ounces strawberries
2 ounces banana
6 ounces orange sherbet
3 ounces crushed ice

Nutritional Information: Serving size 24 oz.
Calories 367
Calories from fat 1.8g
Cholesterol 2%
Total Carbohydrates 91.9g
Protein 2.6g
Fiber 3.3g

Smoothie King

The following smoothie recipes are from private reserve of Steve Kuhnau, CEO and founder of Smoothie King.

The Wing Ding

---

1 cup ripe cantaloupe
1/8 cup turbinado
2 ounces papaya juice
2 cups ice

Classic Watermelon Smoothie

---

2 cups seedless watermelon
1 tablespoon soy protein powder
1 tablespoon honey
1/8 cup turbinado
1 cup crushed ice

The Appleton

---

6 ounces of fresh chopped apples
1/8 cup turbinado
1 tablespoon soy protein powder
2 ounces of papaya juice
1 tablespoon honey
2 cups ice

Produce Juice Recipes

Produce

Vegetable Juice Recipes

Here are some favorite recipes for fresh vegetable drinks. An 8-ounce yield will depend upon the size of the produce and the water content. Use a centrifugal juicer or masticating juicer, unless otherwise noted.

Straight Carrot Juice - *A traditional favorite*

Produce
Use well chilled, pre-soaked juicing carrots.

Notes
Juice until you achieve yield desired.

Carrot Juice & Celery

Produce
Several juicing carrots to yield 7 ounces
1 stalk of fresh celery to yield 1 ounce

Notes
For 8 ounce serving, juice 1 ounce of celery first. Then juice carrots.

Carrot Juice & Apple

Produce
Several juicing carrots to yield 7 ounces
1/2 green Granny Smith apple to yield 1 ounce

Notes
For 8 ounce serving, juice 1 ounce apple first,
then juice carrots.

Carrot Juice & Spinach

Produce
Several juicing carrots to yield 6 ounces
Fresh spinach to yield 2 ounces

Notes
For 8 ounce serving, juice 2 ounce spinach first,
then juice carrots.

Vegi-Combo©

Produce
Several juicing carrots to yield 6 ounces
2" piece of fresh celery
1\4 piece of medium beet
Small piece of onion
1\3 clove of garlic
Small handful of parsley

Notes
For 8-ounce serving, juice produce first, then juice carrots to bring total to 8 ounces.

Carrot & Alfalfa Sprout Juice

Produce
Several juicing carrots to yield 8 ounces
Fresh alfalfa sprouts to yield 1 ounce

Notes
For 8 ounce serving, juice alfalfa sprouts first using a press juicer. Add alfalfa sprout juice to carrot juice.

Straight Alfalfa Sprout Juice

Produce
Enough fresh alfalfa sprouts to yield 1 - 2 ounces of juice.

Notes
Use a wheat-grass juicer (press juice machine)
Juice only enough for 1 - 2 ounce serving. Serve in small 1-2 ounce plastic sauce container

Wheatgrass Juice

Wheatgrass has been steadily growing in popularity for the past several years and even more so recently with the advent of commercial juice bars.

In her book, *The Wheatgrass Book*, Ann Wigmore explains about the benefits of drinking pure grass juice. It is claimed to help rid toxins in the body thereby increasing energy levels. She states, "...Wheatgrass juice stimulates metabolism and bodily enzyme systems in enriching the blood by increasing red blood cell count, and in dilating the blood pathways throughout the body, reducing blood pressure...As a protective food/medicine, wheat grass juice is a storehouse of vitamins, minerals, enzymes, amino acids, and oxygen..."

Wheatgrass Juice

Very strong taste.

Produce
Enough fresh wheat grass to yield 1 ounce of juice

Notes
Use a wheatgrass juicer (press juice machine)
Juice only enough for 1 serving. Serve in small 1-ounce
plastic sauce container

Costing Your Fresh Squeezed Drinks

You can compute the cost of your fresh squeezed drinks by
using the following formula:

Cost per pound X Weight to make = Cost of drink

For example, if you wanted to know the total cost of your 8
ounce carrot drink, and the cost per pound of your carrots is
0.75 cents and the weight to make is 0.50 pounds, then:

0.75 cents X 0.50 pounds = 0.38 cents

Therefore, it will cost 38 cents for an 8 ounce serving of
fresh squeezed carrot juice. You can use the same formula
for drinks that have multiple ingredients. Simply compute the
cost of each portion, then sum the totals of all portions to get
the grand total cost of the drink.

Milk Alternative Recipes

Rice Milk Recipes

Rice Milk Recipe #1

2 cups white rice
4 cups water

Rinse rice to clean. Pour 4 cups of boiling water over rice &
let soak for 1-2 hours. Blend 1 cup soaked rice with 2 1/2
cups water (can be cold water). Blend rice to a slurry (not a
smooth liquid). Pour into a pot & repeat with rest of rice.
Bring to a boil & then reduce heat & simmer for 20
minutes. Line colander with nylon tricot or a few layers of
cheesecloth. Put bowl under colander. Pour rice mix in
colander. Another 1 cup of water (or less or more) can be
poured over the rice to get out more milk. Press with the
back of a spoon and/or twist nylon & squeeze out as much
milk as possible.

This milk is very plain and can be flavored with oil, vanilla,
cinnamon, salt, etc.

Rice Milk Recipe #2

A good way to make rice milk is to use freshly cooked rice that is still hot.

1 cup rice
4 cups hot water
1 teaspoon vanilla
4 teaspoons sugar

Put all in blender. Puree for about 5 minutes (until smooth). Let sit for 1/2 hour. Pour into container, being careful not to let the sediments at the bottom pour into the new container. Strain through cheesecloth.

Soy Milk

Soy Milk Recipe #1

Use one pound of soybeans. Soak for 24 hrs.
Drain soybeans and pour into 2 gallons of filtered water.
Heat until just boiling and sprinkle with cold water to just stop the boiling. Do this 2 more times and then let the beans simmer about 5 minutes. Strain through strainer or cheesecloth.

You now have soy milk. You may adjust the water to make it stronger or weaker as your taste dictates. Add vanilla or honey or almond paste for a flavor.

Soy Milk Recipe #2

I have made soymilk before and you must boil it. After soaking the beans, boil lots of water. Grind the soaked soybeans with the boiling water. (Caution. I use a Vita-Mix for this step). If you don't have a steel blender, use hot water and grind the beans. Be careful to avoid burns. Strain through cheesecloth and then boil the milk. Use soy lecithin and sweetener. Some recipes suggest oil and honey. Chill it and enjoy.

Nut Milk

Nut Milk Recipe #1 - Almond Milk

Start with whole almonds and soak them overnight in water. Next day, blanch the almonds (dip in boiling water) and remove the skins (they come right off). Puree in blender with water and maybe some sweetener and vanilla if you like. Filter out the grit and you have almond milk. Easy!

Nut Milk Recipe #2

1 cup of almonds, freshly roasted
2 1/4 to 4 cups water.

Place the almonds and water (2 1/4 cups for topping or spread, 4 cups for drinking) in a tightly closed jar and store in the refrigerator for 1 to 2 days at the most. Pour into a blender and blend until the mixture is smooth. To use it as a drink, strain first. The remaining almond paste is delicious and can be tossed on cereal, vegetables or rice.

Nut Milk Recipe #3

Put 1/2 cup raw pecans, almonds, cashews, walnuts, Brazil nuts, etc., into a blender container. Process until ground. Add 1/2 cup water and process at low speed for a few seconds, then turn blender to high. Blend for a couple of minutes, then add 1 1/2 cups water. Blend well.

If milk is grainy (almonds and some other nuts and seeds are, but none on the above list), strain through a few layers of cheesecloth. Use the pulp in your next batch of bread. Store in the refrigerator. This is really good stuff, but has quite a bit of fat. Nuts are good food, though, and contain no cholesterol.

Appendix

Appendix

Raw Juice Benefits

For many centuries cultures have used raw juice therapy to help relieve the symptoms of many disorders. Juice can assist conventional medical remedies by helping heal and relieve symptoms. *It is recommended that you use juice therapies to augment any of your medical doctor's advice.*

- **Acne Skin Disorders** - Carrot, lettuce, spinach, beet, cucumber, grape, apricot, green pepper, and raw potato.

- **Allergies** - Carrot, celery, beet, and cucumber.

- **Anemia** - Carrot, beet, celery, spinach, parsley, and watercress.

- **Angina Pectoris** (Slight chest pain) - Carrot, celery, and spinach.

- **Arthritis** - Carrots, celery, beet, and cucumber.

- **Asthma** - Carrots, spinach, celery.

- **Biliousness** (Nausea) - Carrot, spinach, beet, cucumber, celery, and parsley.

- **Bladder Disease** - Carrot, celery, spinach, parsley, cucumber, and beet.

- **Boils and Carbuncles** - Carrot, spinach, beet, and cucumber.

Appendix

- **Bronchitis** - Carrot, spinach, celery, beet, and cucumber.

- **Cancer** - Carrot, celery, spinach, cabbage, and apple.

- **Catarrh** - Carrot, celery, spinach, beet, and cucumber.

- **Colds** - Carrot, celery, lemon, orange, and grapefruit.

- **Colitis** - Carrot, apple, beet, and cucumber.

- **Constipation** - Carrot, apple, celery, spinach, and grape.

- **Dermatitis** - Carrot, celery, apple, beet, and cucumber.

- **Diarrhea** - Carrot, apple, celery, spinach, parsley, raspberry, and blackberry.

- **Eye Diseases** (Due to vitamin deficiency) - Carrot, spinach, celery, and parsley.

- **Gout** - Carrot, celery, spinach, parsley, beet, and cucumber.

- **Halitosis** (Bad Breath) - Carrot, celery, cucumber, and spinach.

- **Hay Fever** - Carrot, celery, beet, cucumber, spinach, and parsley.

- **Headache** - Carrot, spinach, celery, parsley, beet, cucumber, and lettuce.

- **Heart Trouble** (Functional) - Carrot, spinach, celery, parsley, and cucumber.

Appendix

- **High Blood Pressure** - Carrot, cucumber, parsley, spinach, celery, and beet.

- **Influenza** - Carrot, celery, spinach, beet, cucumber, grapefruit, and lemon.

- **Insomnia** - Carrot, spinach, and lettuce.

- **Kidney Trouble** - Lemon, carrot, dandelion, parsley, spinach, celery, beet, cucumber, and grape.

- **Liver Disorders** - Carrot, beet, parsley, cucumber, dandelion, and radish.

- **Malainse** - Carrot, celery, apple, beet, cucumber, and parsley.

- **Migraine Headache** - Carrot, spinach, celery, and parsley.

- **Mucous Membrane** - Carrot, apple, pineapple, celery, beet, and cucumber.

- **Nerve Disorders** - Lettuce, carrot, celery, apple, spinach, cucumber, beer, and radish.

- **Overweight** - Carrot, celery, spinach, beet, and cucumber.

- **Peptic Ulcer** - Cabbage, celery, and carrot.

- **Rheumatism** - Carrot, celery, spinach, parsley, lettuce, watercress, and cucumber.

- **Rickets** - Carrots, celery, spinach, apple, orange, lemon, and grapefruit.

Appendix

- **Scurvy** - Carrot, celery, apple, grapefruit, orange, and lemon.

- **Sinus Trouble** - Carrot, spinach, beet, and cucumber.

- **Toxemia** - Carrot, parsley, celery, spinach, cucumber, and apple.

- **Tuberculosis** - Carrot, alfalfa sprouts, parsley, spinach, and watercress.

Source: Diet for Health

Information Sources

With the deregulation of the telephone industry, prefixes for phone numbers change rapidly. Websites are much more stable. They provide up-to-date contact information and in-depth information. Therefore, to keep contact information from going obsolete, website addresses are offered.

The Juice & Smoothie Association
C/O Juice Gallery
Phone: (909) 597-0791

Website address: *www.smoothiecentral.com*

The Juice & Smoothie Association is a marketing entity established to promote the juice and smoothie industry worldwide. The association offers reports, training materials and a newsletter called, *The Juice Review* .

Juice Gallery
Chino Hills, California
Phone: (909) 597-0791

Website address: *www.juicegallery.com*

Juice Gallery is a multimedia publishing and restaurant consulting firm that concentrates on the business needs of the specialty foodservice industry. The company publishes books, reports, and software about the smoothie, wrap, gourmet coffee, and bagel industries.

Appendix

Government Educational Websites

National Institute of Health

Website address: *www.odp.hih.gov*

The NIH operates a website that is full of valuable information. The site includes the International Bibliographical Information on Dietary Supplements (IBIDS), which is a database of published, international, scientific literature on dietary supplements, including vitamins, minerals, and botanicals.

The Food and Nutrition Information Center
Sponsored by The United States Department of Agriculture (USDA).

Website address: *www.nal.usda.gov/fnic/*

The Food and Nutrition Information Center (FNIC) is one of several information centers at the National Agricultural Library (NAL), part of the United States Department of Agriculture's (USDA), Agricultural Research Service (ARS). You can access all the FNIC's resource lists and databases, as well as many other food and nutrition related web sites from this award winning site.

Appendix

The Food and Drug Administration
Center for Food Safety & Applied Nutrition (CFSAN)

Website address: *http://vm.cfsan.fda.gov/*

The FDA is the Untied States oldest consumer protection agency, charged with protecting American consumers by enforcing the Federal Food, Drug, and Cosmetic Act and several related public health laws. Their web site is a great place to get educated about food laws and to get up to date information regarding issues about food and beverages.

World Health Organization (WHO)

Web site address: *www.who.int/*

The world press and media seem to have high confidence in The World Health Organization. Their quotes and statistics are mentioned all the time by the main stream press. The basic question is: WHO is WHO? Their agenda follows:

The World Health Organization attempts to direct and coordinate authority on international health work and strives to bring the highest level of health to all peoples. WHO proposes conventions, agreements, regulations and makes recommendations about international nomenclature of diseases, causes of death, and public health practices. It develops, establishes, and promotes international standards concerning foods, biological , pharmaceutical, and similar substances.

One has to question the viability of such an aggressive agenda. It is difficult enough for the United States Food and Drug Administration to provide information and oversee

Appendix

health concerns for states, county, and local health administrators within the United States. How can an international organization seek to oversee the health concerns of the entire planet? - Another question is: WHO reports to WHO? - Check out their web site for more information. Most importantly, be aware of WHO they are.

Metric Conversion Table

If you use metric measurements when you cook, use the following table to convert the measurements for the recipes in this book:

Volume	Metric Measure (in milliliters)
1/4 teaspoon	1.25
1/2 teaspoon	2.5
1 teaspoon	5
1 tablespoon	15
1/4 cup	60
1/3 cup	80
1/2 cup	125
3/4 cup	180
1 cup	250

Juice & Smoothie Companies

Get the *scoop* on the juice & smoothie companies that appear in this book by visiting their websites. You will get information about the companies and contact information for ordering products. Here is their main office information:

Jamba Juice
1700 17th Street
San Francisco, CA 94103
Phone (415) 865-1100
Web *www.jambajuice.com*

Juice It Up!
One Corporate Park, Suite 150
Irvine, CA 92606
Phone (949) 475-0146
Fax (949) 633-1018
Web *www.juiceitup.com*

California Juice Stop
23120 Alicia Parkway, Suite 200
Mission Viejo, CA 92692
Phone (949) 707-4617
Fax (949) 707-1383
www.quikpage.com

Juice Kitchen
1050 17th Street, Suite B195
Denver, CO 80265
Phone (303) 573-7060
Web *www.juicekitchen.com*

Planet Smoothie
One Buckhead Plaza
3060 Peachtree Road, Suite 340
Atlanta, GA 30305
Phone (404) 239-0009
Web *www.planetsmoothie.com*

Robeks Juice
2736 Main Street
Santa Monica, CA 90405
Phone (310) 581-0700
Toll Free 1-888-ROBEKS
Fax (310) 581-0660
Web *www.robeksjuice.com*

Smoothie King
2400 Veterans Blvd. Suite 110
Kenner, LA 70062
Phone (504) 467-4006
Fax (504) 469-1274
Web *www.smoothieking.com*

Bibliography

Bibliography

Back to Eden, by Jethro Kloss. Published by Back to Eden Books, Loma Linda, California.

The Juicing Book, by Stephen Blauer. Published by Avery Publishing Group, Garden City Park, New York.

Juicing For Life, by Cherie Calbom and Maureen Keane. Published by Avery Publishing Group, Garden City Park, New York.

Survival Into The 21st Century, by Viktoras Kulvinskas. Published by 21st Century Publications, Fairfield, Iowa.

The Wheatgrass Book, by Ann Wigmore. Published by Avery Publishing Group, Garden City Park, New York.

Nutrition: The Cancer Answer, by Mareen Salaman. Published by Statford Press, Menlo Park, California.

Life and Health, by Samual Howard. Published by Random House Publications.

Medical Aid Encyclopedia, Edited by Leroy E. Burney. Published by Royal Publishers, Nashville, Tennessee.

Index

Index

Index

Index

My Smoothie Recipes

My Smoothie Recipes

My Smoothie Recipes

My Smoothie Recipes

My Smoothie Recipes

My Smoothie Recipes

EQUIPMENT AND SOFTWARE

ORDER DIRECT BY TELEPHONE
OR VIA THE WEB

(909) 597-0791
www.juicegallery.com

VISA - MASTERCARD - AMEX

♦*MIRACLE ELECTRIC WHEAT GRASS JUICER,*
Model MJ550
The first and best electric wheat grass juicer for home use,
MJ550, has been upgraded with a more powerful motor
and safety overload switch, so it won't overheat. Great for
wheat grass, soft fruits, and berries.
$174.95

♦*SALAD MAKER ATTACHMENT, Model MJ550ASL*
Three reversible stainless steel slicer and shredder blade
attachments for salads, vegetables and cheese expand the
versatility of the MJ550 electric wheat grass juicer.
$59.95

◆MIRACLE JUICER, Model MJ 1000

This versatile vegetable and fruit juice extractor automatically ejects pulp into an external, removable bin for uninterrupted juicing. Its high-speed motor produces dry pulp for higher juice yield, and its wide hopper aids feeding of small fruits and berries.
$124.95

◆BLENDER ATTACHMENT, Model MJ1000BL

Blender attachment for Miracle Juicer MJ1000.
$23.95

◆MANUAL WHEAT GRASS JUICER, Model MJ400

Easy to use and economical. This practical juice extractor is for wheat grass, soft fruits, berries and leafy vegetables. Its rugged tin plated cast iron construction and stainless steel screen provide long life and easy cleaning.
$57.95

◆PROFESSIONAL MIRACLE WHEAT GRASS JUICER, Model MJ475

This rugged extractor is the Pro at juicing wheat grass and soft fruits. Its juicing parts are made of finely finished cast iron and its two interchangeable strainer screens are stainless steel. No aluminum parts. Its three-way switch allows choice of two speeds and pulse action from its strong 450 watt, 60 cycle motor. Available in 220 voltage.
$549.95

◆MIRACLE ULTRA-MATIC® JUICE EXTRACTOR
Model MJ7000-1
Stainless Steel inside and out, this is the most technologically advanced model with automatic pulp ejection. Boasting a 450 watt motor and oversized pulp ejector, it handles fruit and vegetables - even leafy ones - easily - for a non-stop flow of fresh juice.
$349.95

◆MIRACLE SOY WONDER, Model MJ717
Automatically makes over 2 quarts of ready-to-use soy milk from soybeans in just 22 minutes! Simply insert soaked soy beans, add water, switch on, and it's done. Its controlled cooking and grinding process produces a delicious soy milk without a "beany" taste at a fraction of the cost of packaged soy products. Recipe book included.
$269.95

◆HANGING WHEATGRASS GROWER, Model MEI05
This ingenious large volume sprouter is great for wheat grass and also dehydrates food naturally without electricity. Its removable shelves give 5 square feet of sprouting or drying. $59.95

◆BIOSTA THREE-TIER SPROUTERS
Models ME85 & ME95
Simple and fool-proof, these sprouters boast three beds and a drain basin. The patented capillary action valves maintain precisely correct germinating water level with one initial watering. ME85 is clear; ME95 is green.
Please specify color when ordering
$24.95

◆ TERRA COTTA SPROUTERS
Models ME60 & ME65

Utilizing the porous quality of terra cotta which controls moisture and a simple tray rotation process, these stacking sprouters produce a daily supply of perfect sprouts. From Germany. ME 60 is 6" high,'5-1/2" in diameter: $39.95: ME 65 is 9-1/2" high, 6-1/4" in diameter: $59.95

 **Give the Gift of Vitality and Health to Your Loved Ones, Friends and Colleagues**

CHECK YOUR LEADING BOOK STORE OR ORDER HERE

Yes, I want____ copies of *Smoothies! The Original Smoothie Book Recipes From the Pro's* at $16.95 each for domestic; $19.95 foreign, plus $4.00 shipping per book (California residents please add $1.27 tax per book). Canadian and foreign orders must be accompanied by a postal money order in U.S. funds, if not paying by credit card. Allow 15 days for delivery.

My check or money order for $_____ is enclosed.
Please charge my:
____ Visa ___Mastercard ___Amex

Name	
Organization	
Address	
City/State/Zip	
Phone	
Email	

Card Number_____
Expiration Date_____
Name on Card_____
Signature of Card Holder_____

Please make check or money order payable and return to:

Juice Gallery
P.O. Box 151
Chino Hills, California 91709

Call/Fax your credit card order to: (909) 597-0791
Place your credit card order online @
www.juicegallery.com

ABOUT THE AUTHOR

Dan Titus, popularly know as *The Smoothieman*, began his quest for the perfect smoothie years ago when he used to tour as a drummer. The rigors of the road made it difficult to eat right. He began packing a blender and juicer along for the tour dates and found that it was well worth the effort to squeeze fresh juice and blend smoothies on the road. A nutritional advocate, he began to spread the word about health and vitality. In 1992, Dan started Juice Gallery, a multimedia publishing and restaurant consulting firm, concentrating on the needs of the specialty foodservice industry.

Juice Gallery, *(www.juicegallery.com)*, is the world authority in regards to research and media information about the juice/smoothie business. The firm has provided industry analysis and reports to eager audiences. This information has helped propel the industry from a simple fade into a solid trend. The firm has captured a market niche, which has helped hundreds of entrepreneurs and corporations realize their goals. The firms customer and client list includes many major players in the foodservice and media industry. For example: Quaker Oats Corporation, General Mills, Corporation, Hunt-Wesson Foods, Del Monte Food Corporation, Kraft Food Corporation, The Coca-Cola Company.

Juice Gallery is a progressive and technically oriented company. The company was the first player in the industry to embrace a new technology called "The Internet", as early as 1994. The company also develops software, videos and other media products, which further differentiates its product mix.

In April 1995, Juice Gallery launched the first trade publication for the juice & smoothie bar industry: *The Juice Review Newsletter.*

The company established *The Juice & Smoothie Association, in December 1998 (www.smoothiecentral.com)*, an organization dedicated to promoting the juice & smoothie industry.

Mail to:

P.O. Box 151
Chino Hills CA 91709

Enter to win
your spot in history!

Simply send us your favorite smoothie recipe, and you could be selected to be placed in future copies of this book. Imagine your name in print for all the world to see!

Name_____

Address_____

_____

City_____ State_____ Zip_____

Phone_____

Email _____

Yes, here is my recipe!

Drink name:_____

_____

_____

_____

_____

_____

_____

_____

_____

_____

_____